Vision Board
Clip Art Book
for Black Women

Copyright © 2024 J. B. Allen
All rights reserved. No portion of this book may be reproduced in any form without permission from the publisher, except as permitted by U.S. copyright law. For permissions contact: hello@myvisionboardbooks.com

"You may not control all the events that happen to you, but you can decide not to be reduced by them." - Maya Angelou

"Turn your wounds into wisdom."
-Oprah Winfrey

"If they don't give you a seat at the table, bring a folding chair." -Shirley Chisholm

"Success isn't about how much money you make; it's about the difference you make in people's lives."
-Michelle Obama

"I have learned over the years that when one's mind is made up, this diminishes fear; knowing what must be done does away with fear." - Rosa Parks

"Power is not given to you. |You have to take it."
Beyoncé

Unveiling Your Vision –
A Journey of Empowerment and Dreams

Black Queens,

Have you ever imagined a life where your deepest desires and aspirations are not just fleeting thoughts but a vivid blueprint for your future?

Welcome to your journey of self-discovery and empowerment. This book is more than just a collection of images and quotes; it's a tool for visualizing your dreams and turning them into realities.

Within these pages lies the power to redefine your future. Each element you choose is a reflection of your desires, a bold statement of your aspirations. This is where you start crafting the life you've always imagined.

Remember, there are no limits here—only possibilities. Let each selection resonate with your heart's truest intentions. Your vision board is not just an artistic creation; it's a roadmap to your aspirations, a daily reminder of your potential and purpose.

So, begin with an open heart. Be brave, be bold, and most importantly, be you.
Your journey to greatness starts here.
Your motivating cheerleader,

J.B. Allen

CATEGORIES

SELF-CARE / MINDFULNESS

HEALTH / WELLNESS / MINDFUL EATING

BEAUTY / FASHION CULTURAL IDENTITY

RELATIONSHIPS / COMMUNICATION

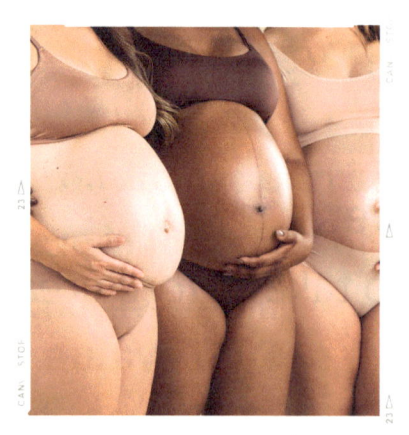

FAMILY / PARENTING

PETS

HOBBIES / CREATIVITY

WORK LIFE BALANCE

SPIRITUALITY / FAITH

CATEGORIES

DAILY HABITS

EDUCATION/ CAREER/

ENTREPRENEURSHIP /DIGITAL MARKETING

FINANCIAL FREEDOM

HOME DECOR/ DECLUTTERING

TRAVEL & ADVENTURE

ENVIRONMENT/ ECO-CONSCIOUS

CHARITY/ VOLUNTEERING

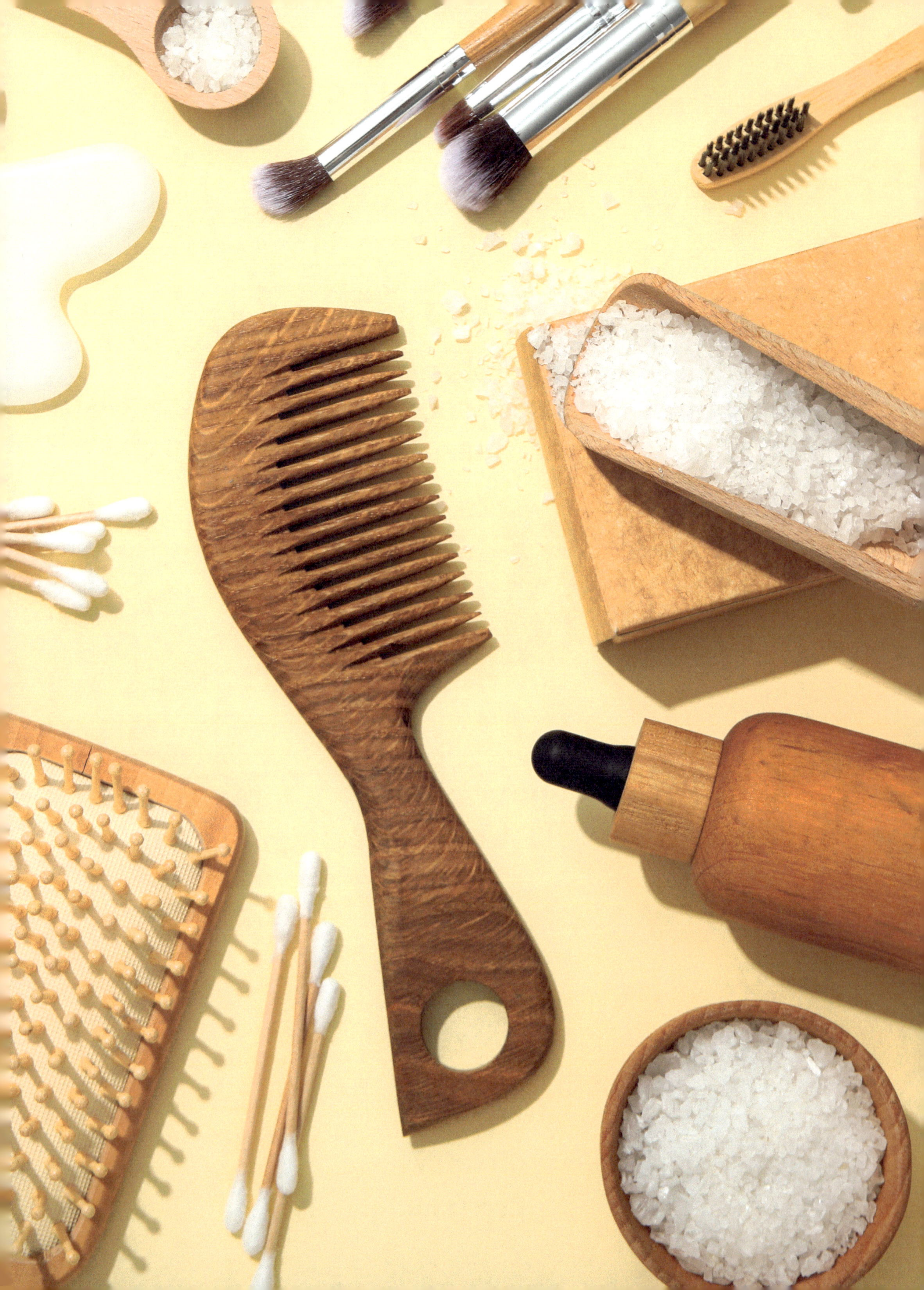

SELF CARE

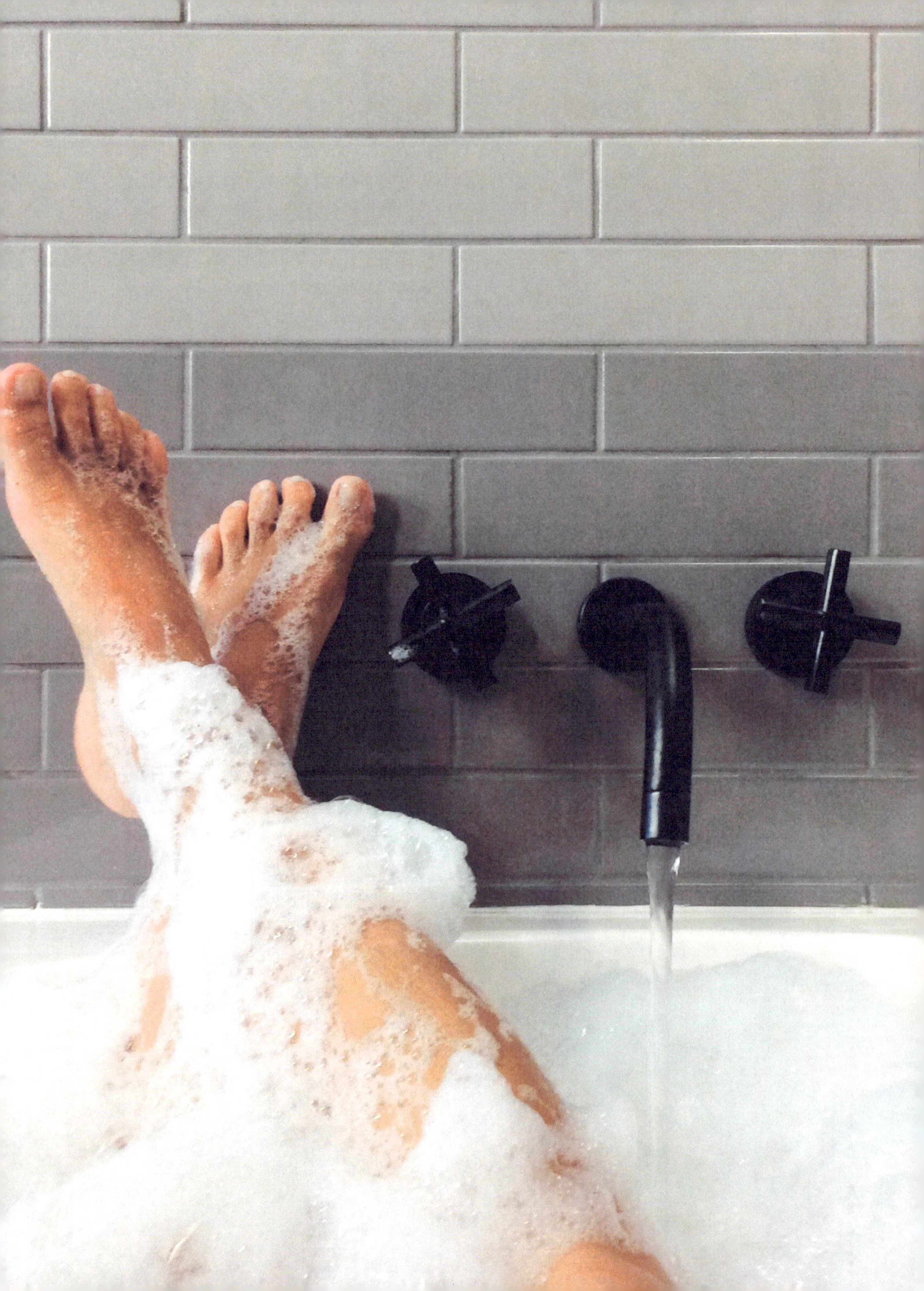

SELF CARE
ISN'T
SELFISH

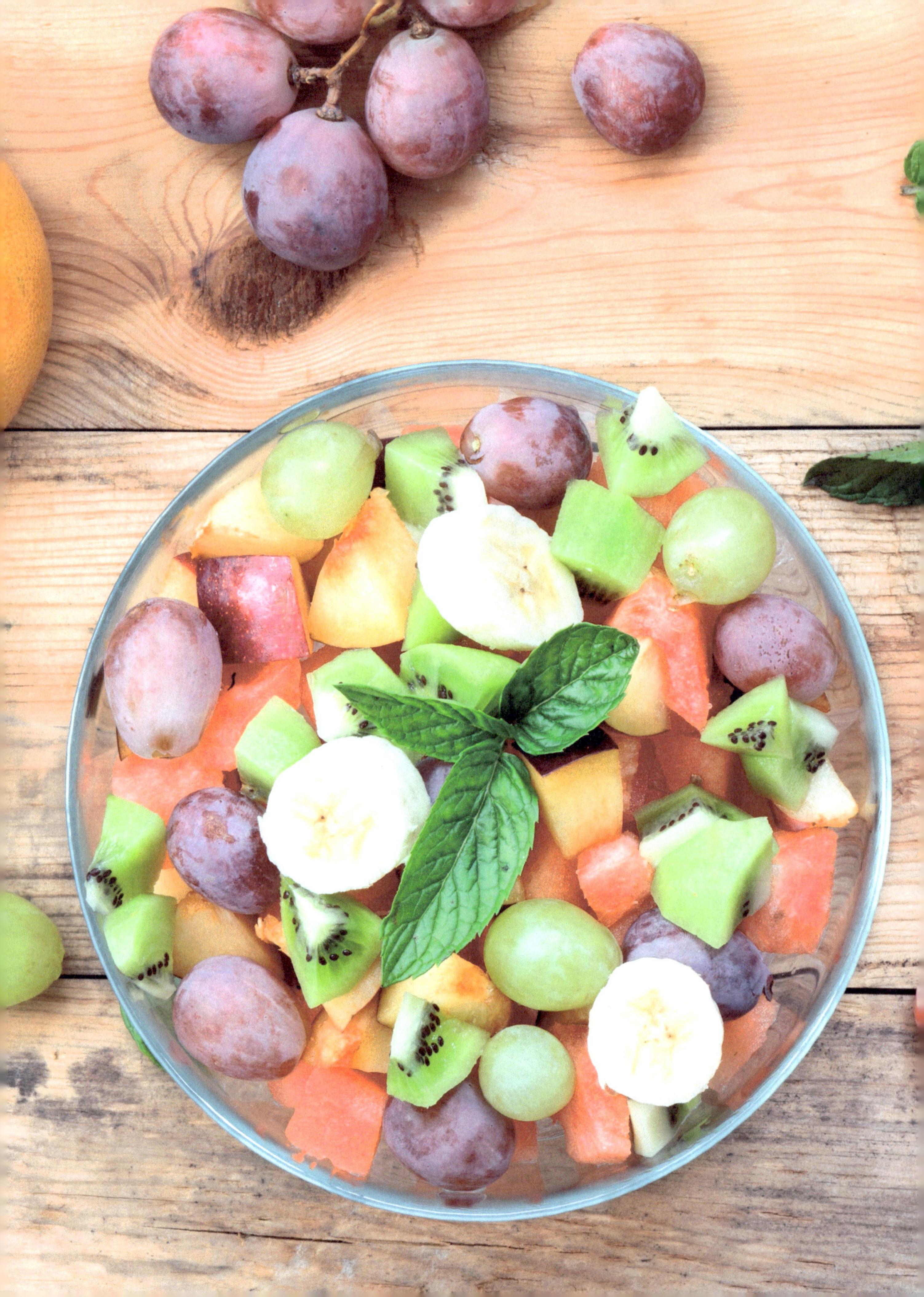

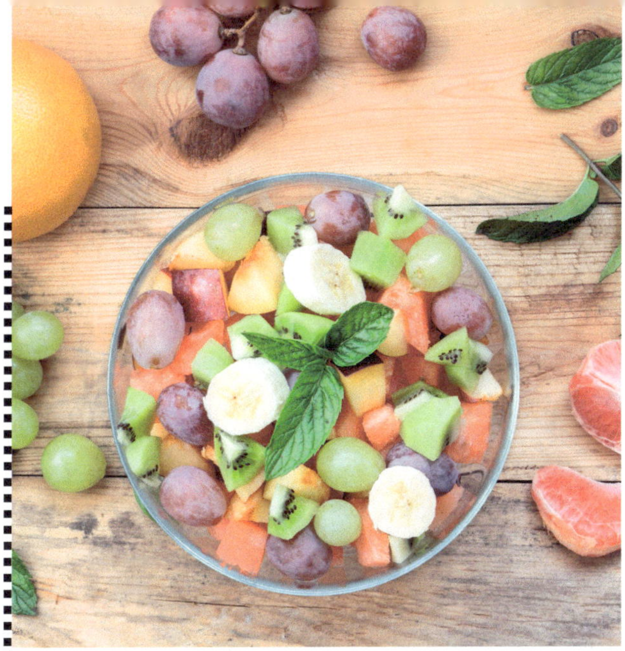
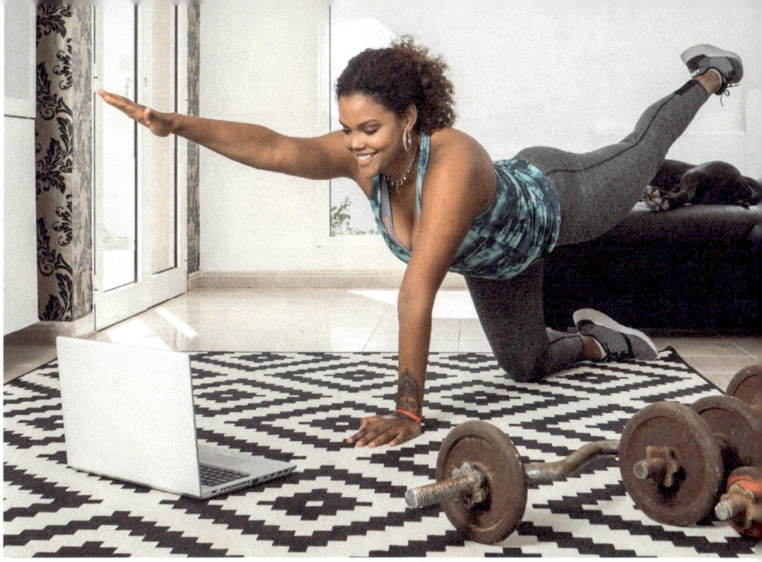
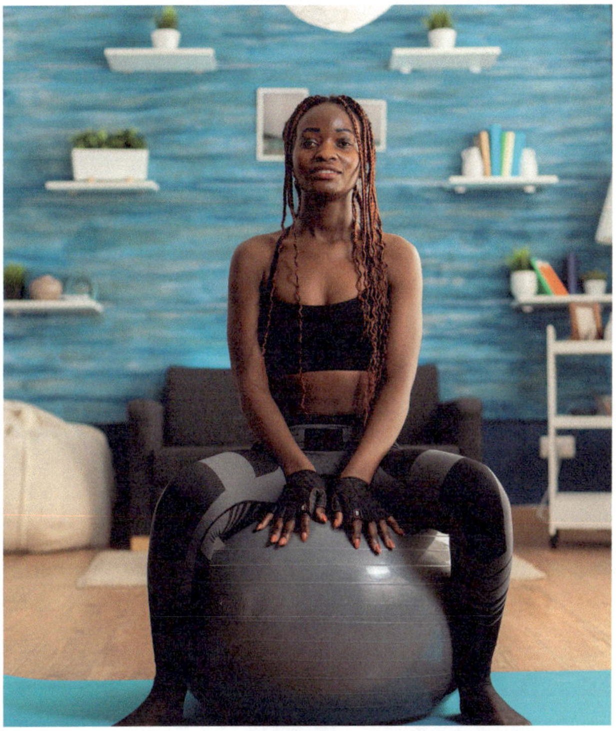
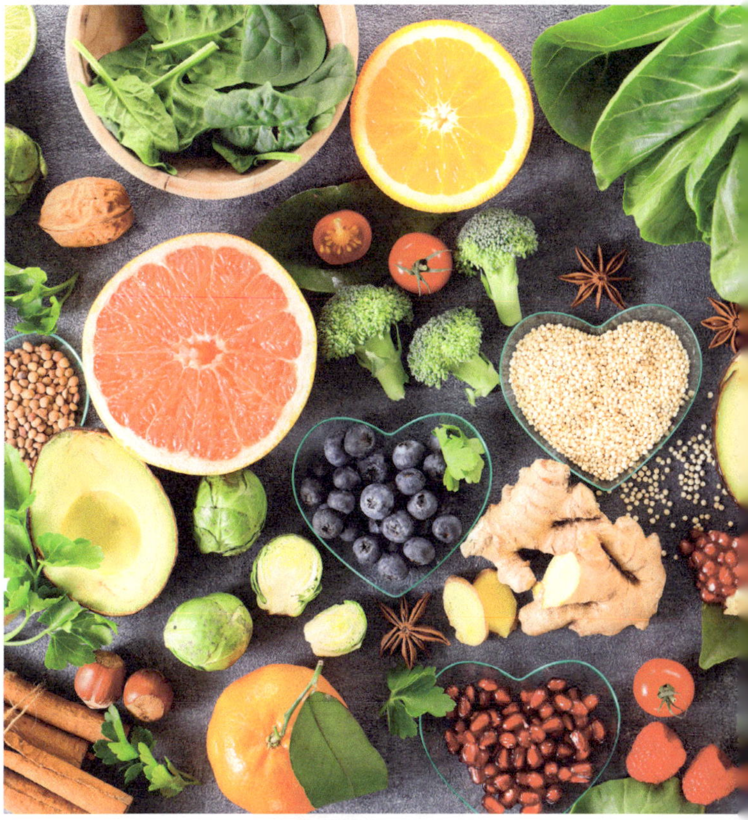
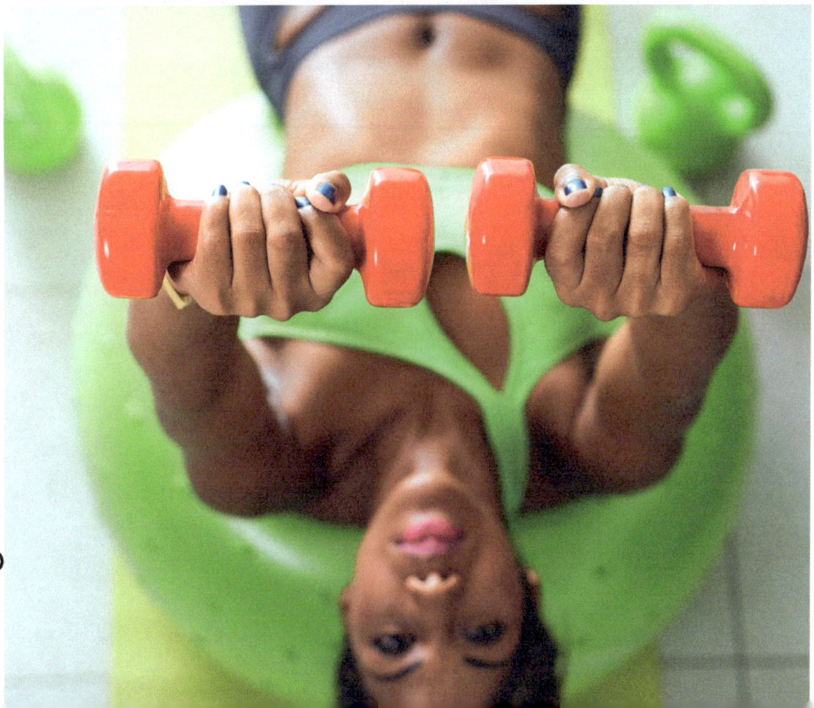
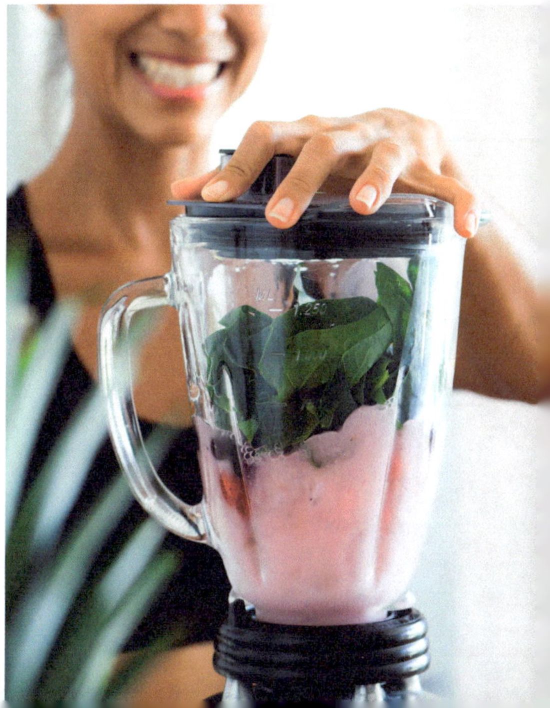

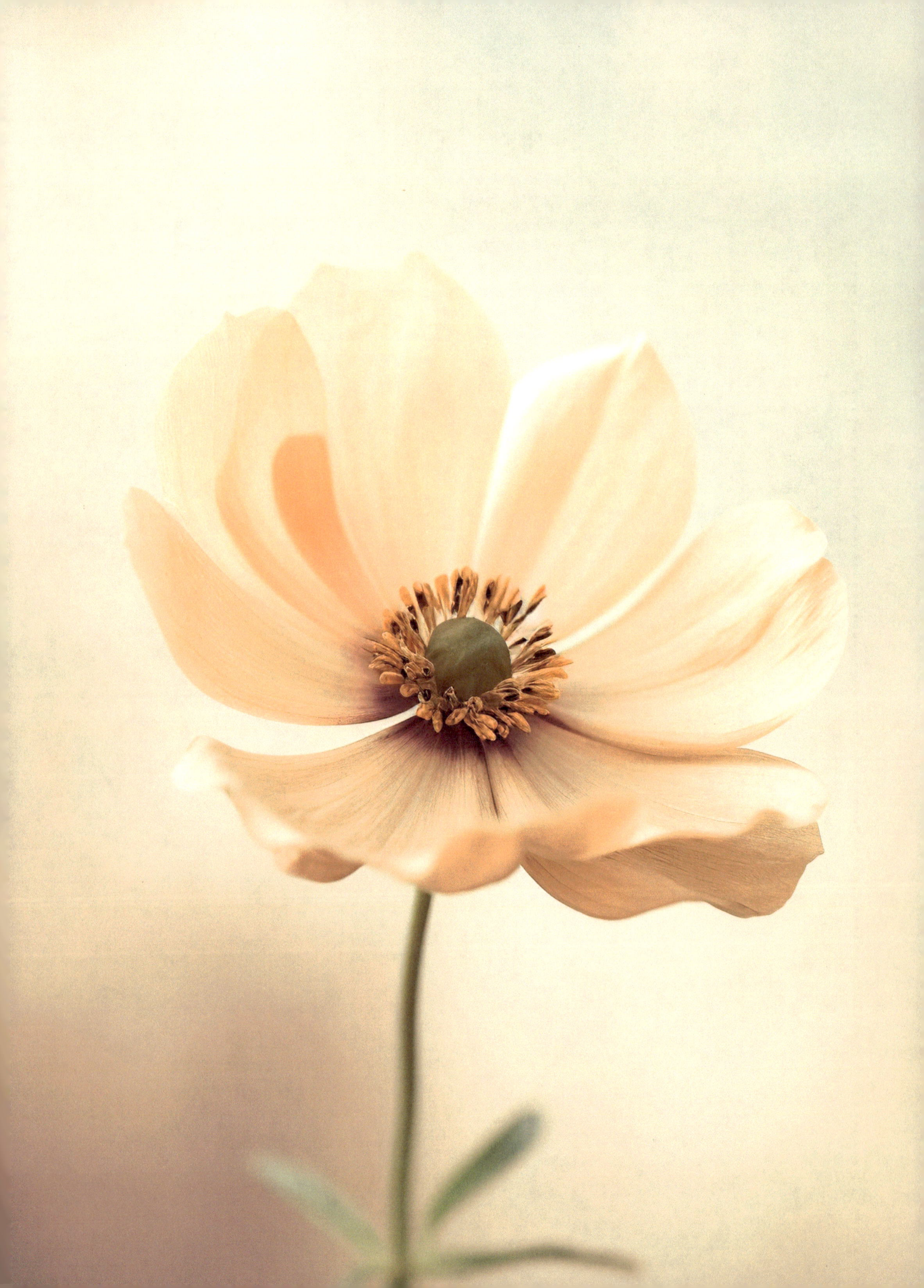

- EMBRACE.
- EMPOWER.
- ELEVATE.

NEVER give up

SELF LOVE

Good Things Take Time

Stay Positive

Love Yourself

Stay Focused

Do It FOR YOU

You are OUT of this WORLD

DREAM BIG

Stay Consistent

All things are Possible

Focus on the present because the present is a gift.

I am beautiful I am loved

KEEP going

Soul Searching Ahead

Wellness Wisdom

"Caring for myself is not self-indulgence; it is self-preservation, and that is an act of political warfare." - Audre Lorde.

How can prioritizing your health be seen as an act of self-love and empowerment, and what steps can you take to make self-care a regular part of your life?

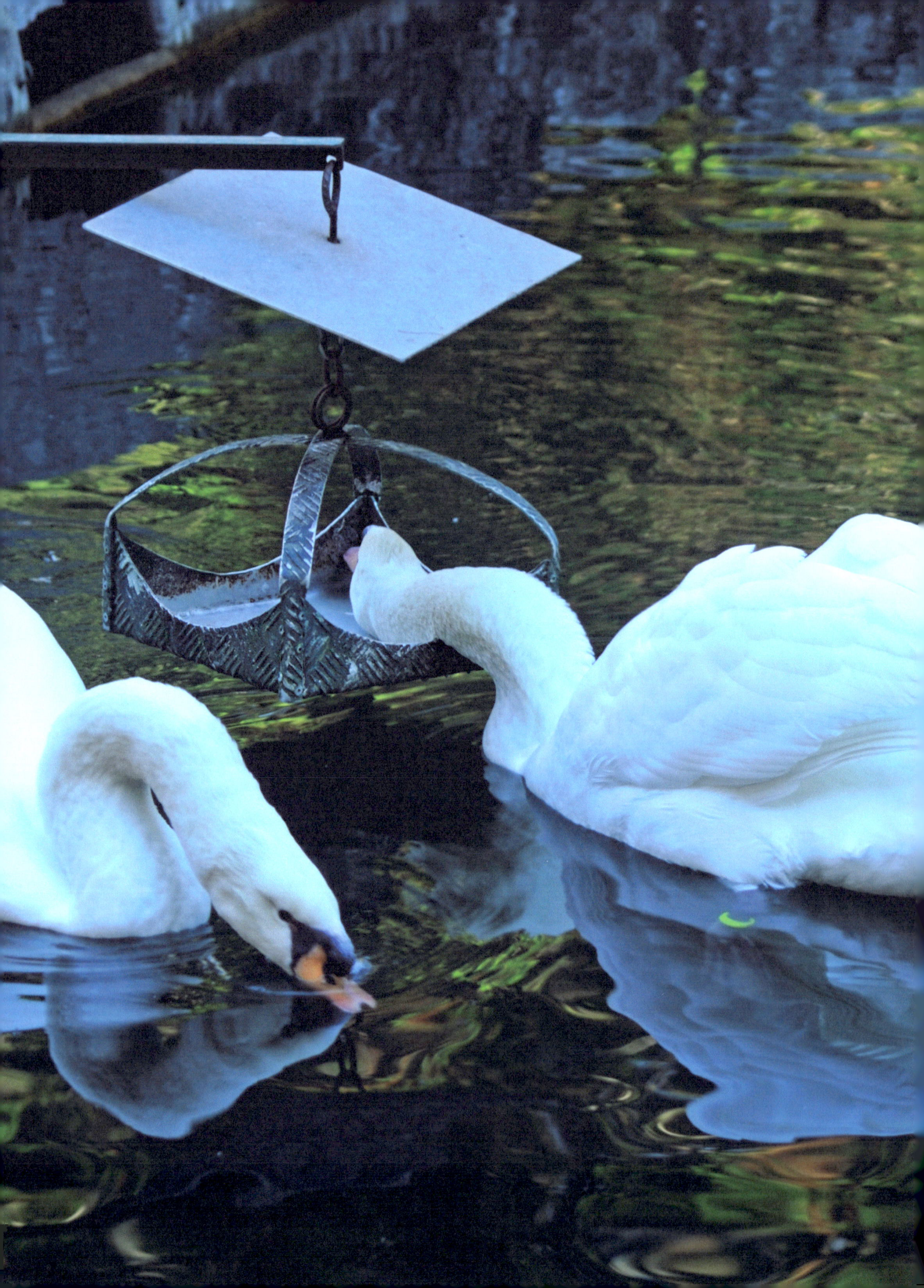

- She BELIEVED She COULD So, She DID
- I AM THE DRIVER OF MY DESTINY, NOT THE PASSENGER. 
- I AM CLOTHED IN STRENGTH AND DIGNITY AND LAUGH WITHOUT FEAR OF THE FUTURE
- The question isn't who's going to let me; it's who is going to stop me. — Ayn Rand    
- LITTLE BY LITTLE, DAY BY DAY, WHAT IS MEANT FOR ME WILL FIND ITS WAY.
- I AM AT PEACE WITH ALL THAT HAS HAPPENED, IS HAPPENING, AND WILL HAPPEN
- I am a powerhouse. I Am indestructible
- I acknowledge my own self-worth; my confidence is soaring
- She remembered who she was, and the game changed. — Lalah Delia
- I AM WORTHY OF ALL THE GOOD THINGS THAT HAPPEN IN MY LIFE
- Fall seven times, stand up eight
- I TURNED MY Cants INTO Cans AND MY Dreams INTO Plans

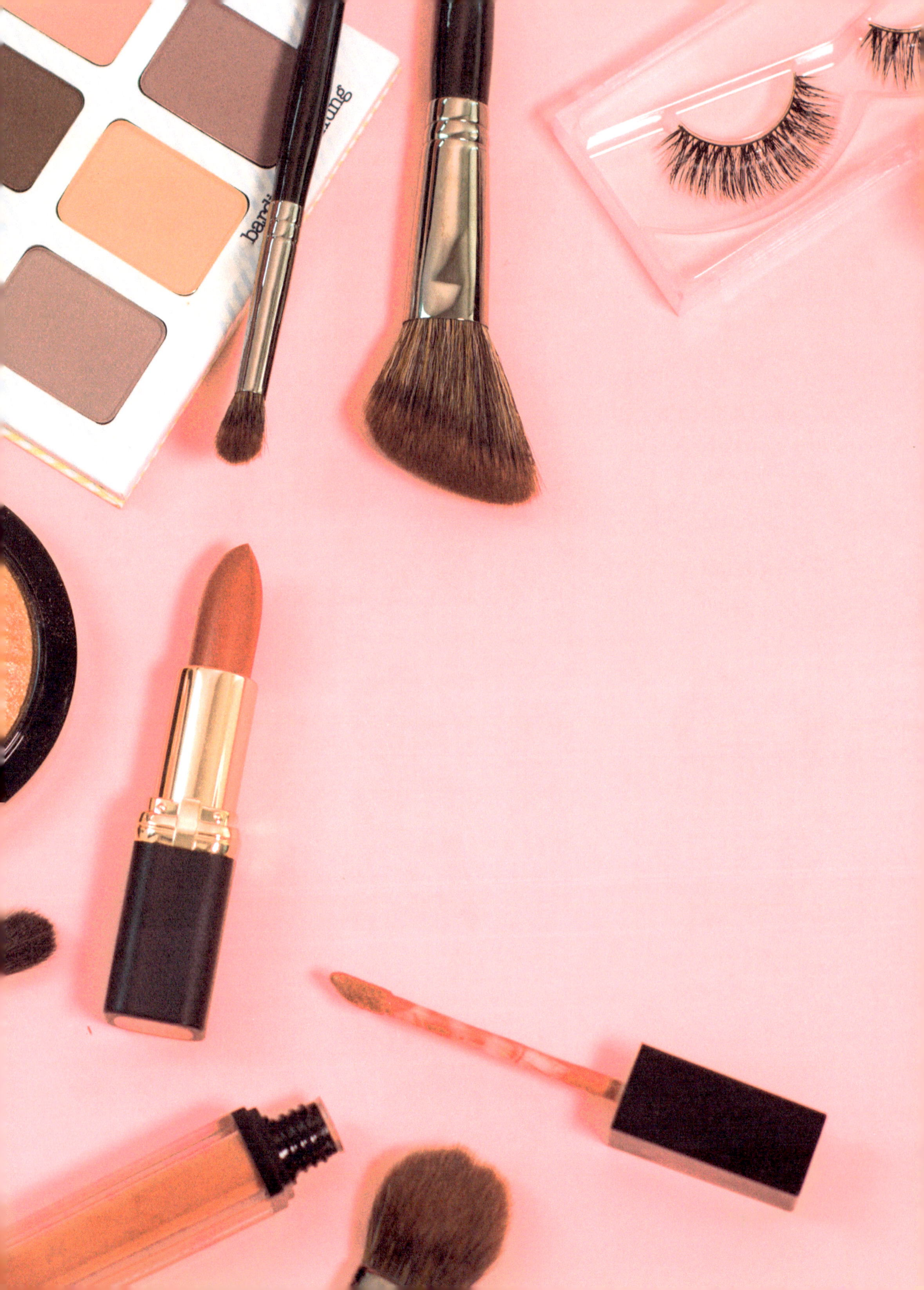

I am *everything*

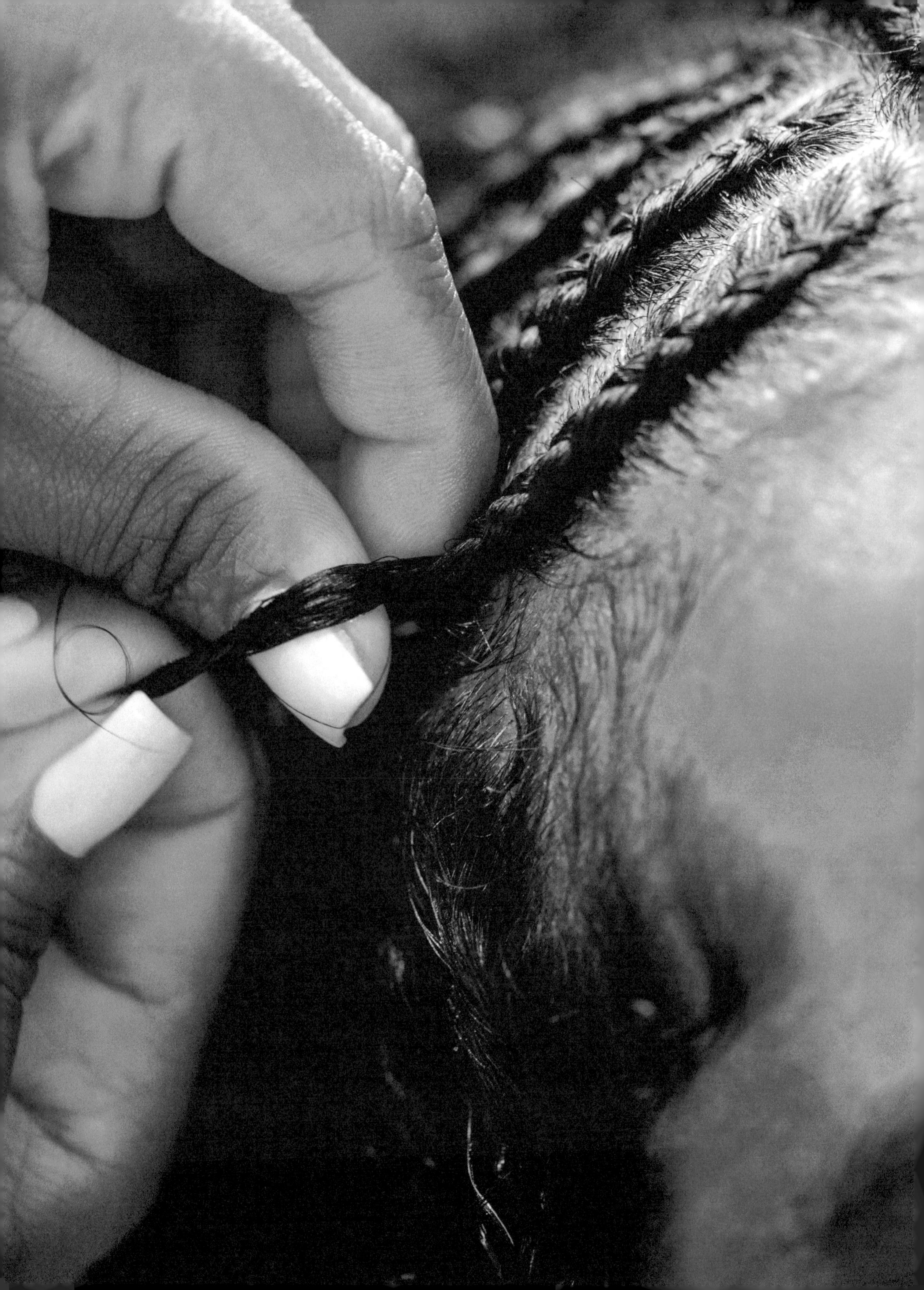

"Black is bold, black is beautiful, black is gold." - Unknown

I ♥ ME

- Dreams and dedication are a powerful combinations
- EVERY CHALLENGE IS AN OPPORTUNITY FOR GROWTH
- THE MOST EFFECTIVE WAY TO DO IT IS TO DO IT — AMELIA EARHART
- MY LIFE ISN'T MINE IF I ALWAYS CARE WHAT OTHERS THINK
- IN THE WORLD OF A MOTHER, A CHILD'S LAUGHTER IS THE MOST PRECIOUS MELODY AND THEIR TEARS THE HEAVIEST BURDEN
- DON'T BE AFRAID TO BE THE FULL PACKAGE
- Where there is no struggle, there is no strength.
- TURN YOUR WOUNDS INTO WISDOM - OPRAH WINFREY
- MOTHERHOOD IS THE EXQUISITE INCONVENIENCE OF BEING ANOTHER PERSON'S EVERYTHING
- BELIEVE YOU CAN, AND YOU'RE HALFWAY THERE
- YOU BECOME WHAT YOU BELIEVE
- You DON'T NEED TO BE AN EXPERT TO DO SOMETHING GREAT

FRIENDSHIP

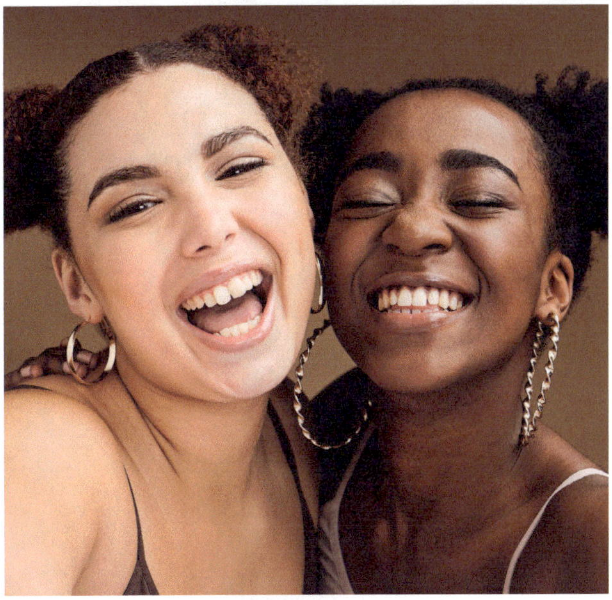
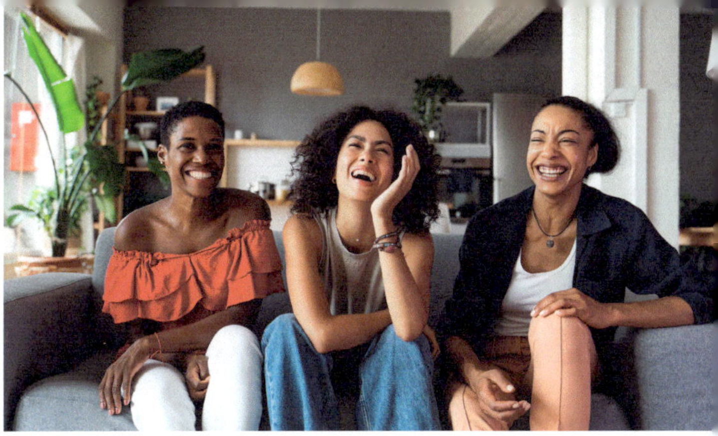
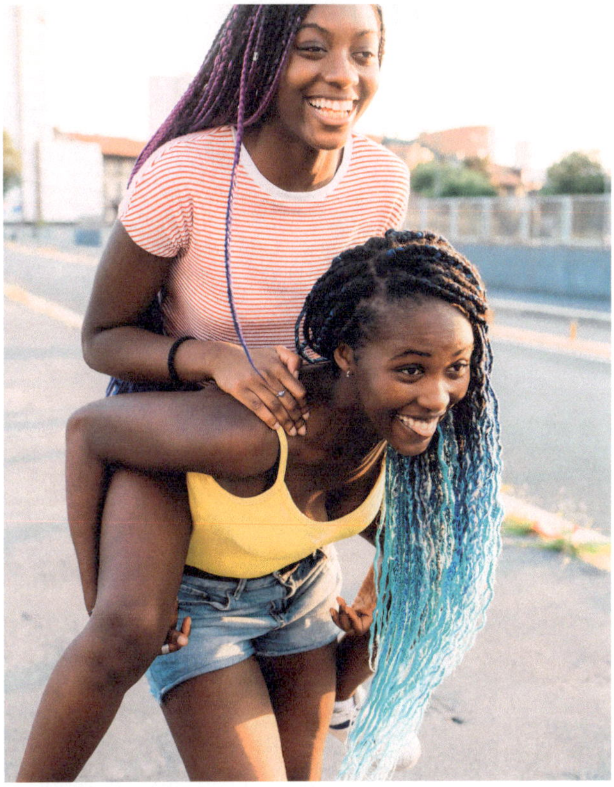
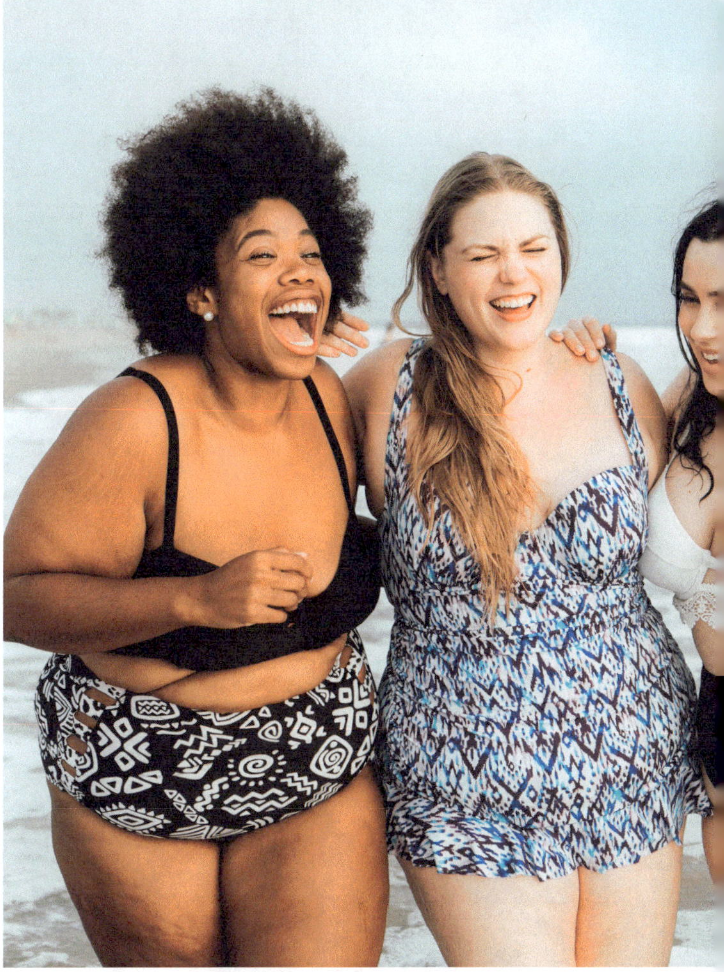
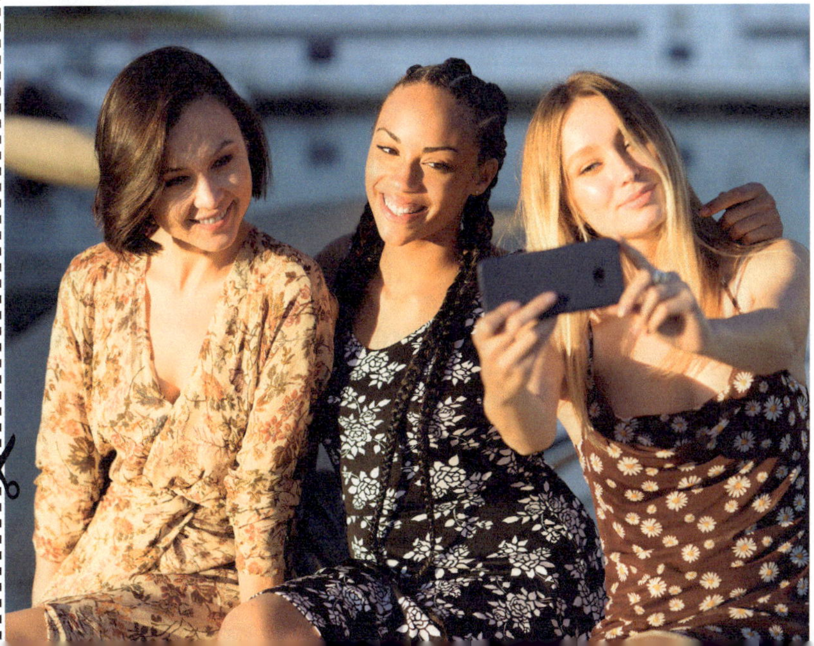
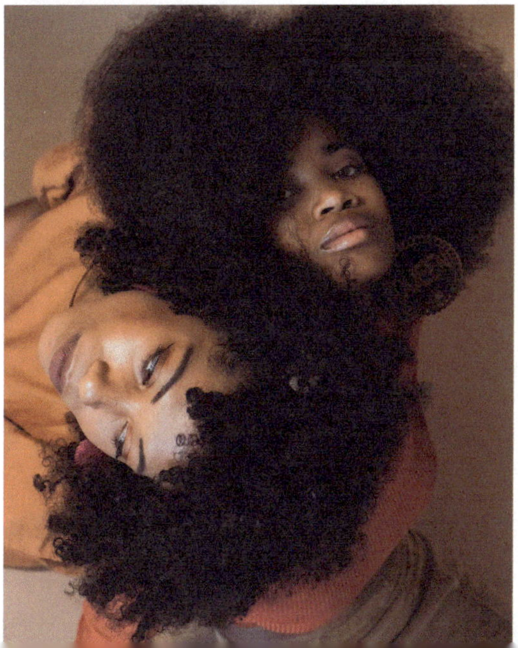

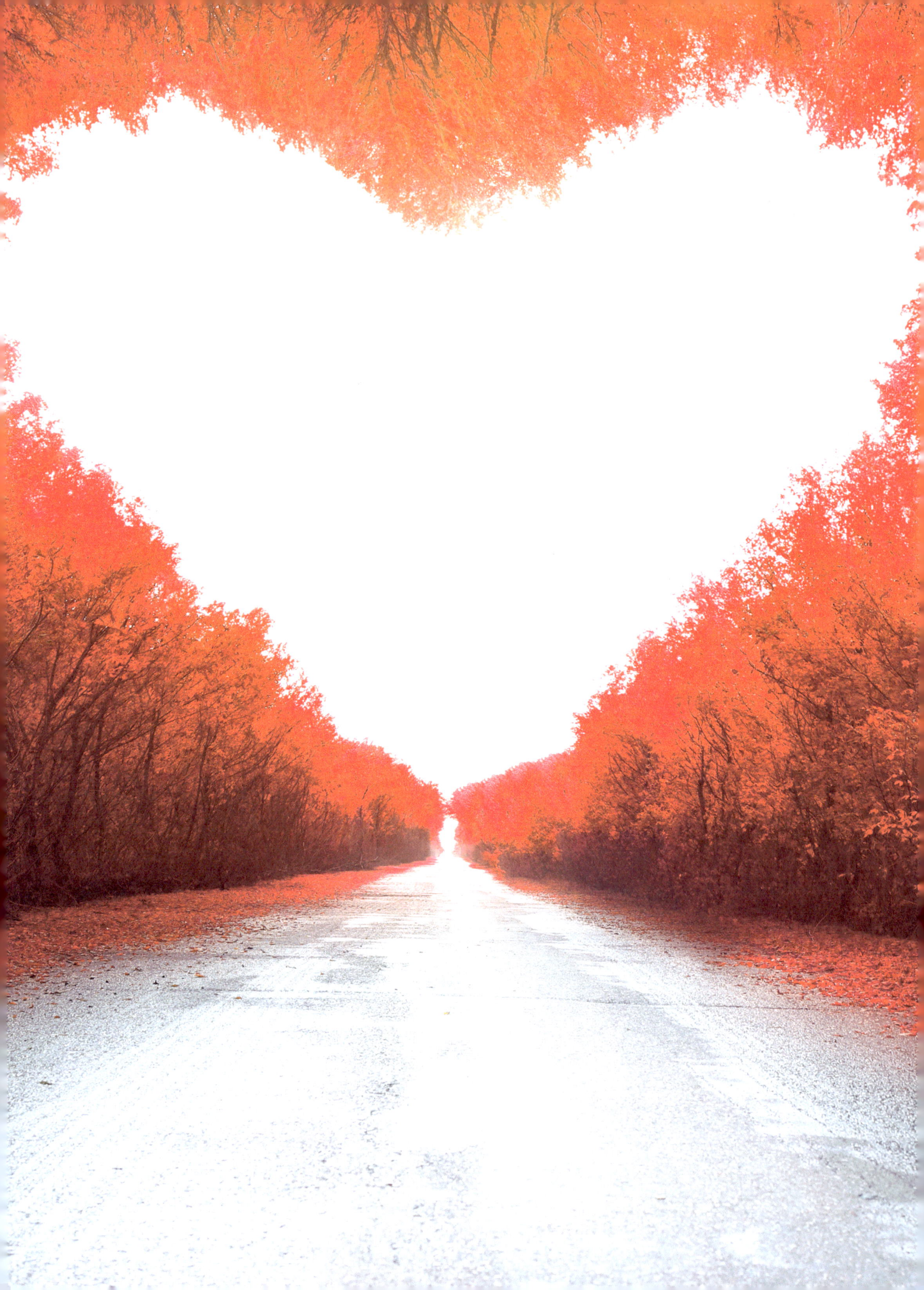

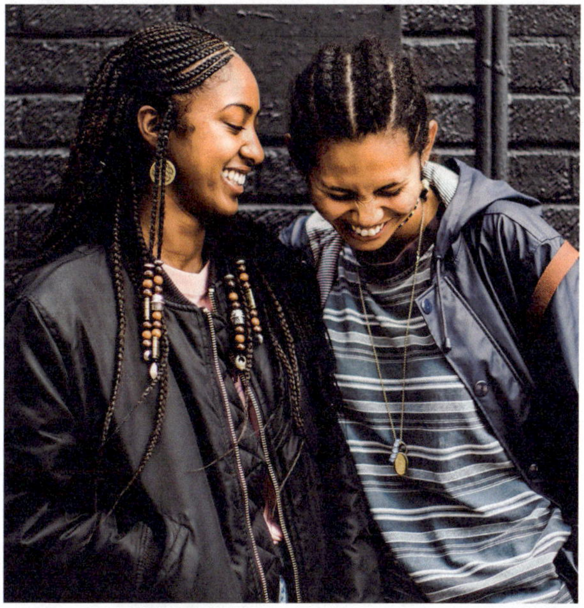
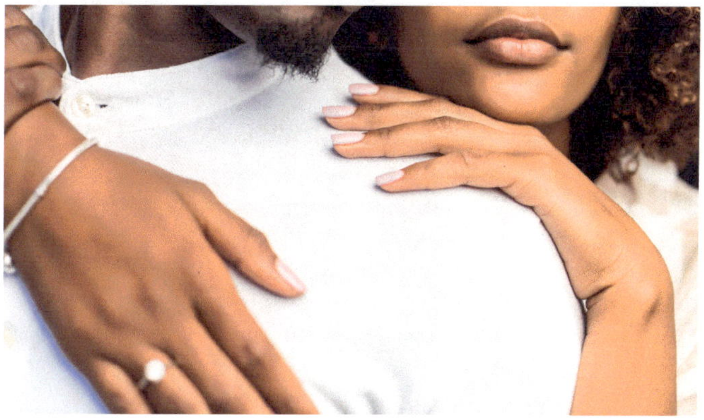
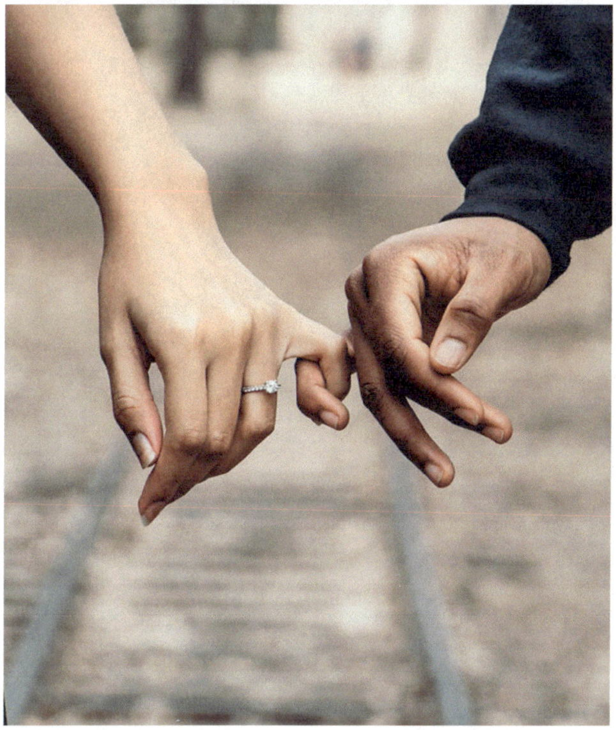
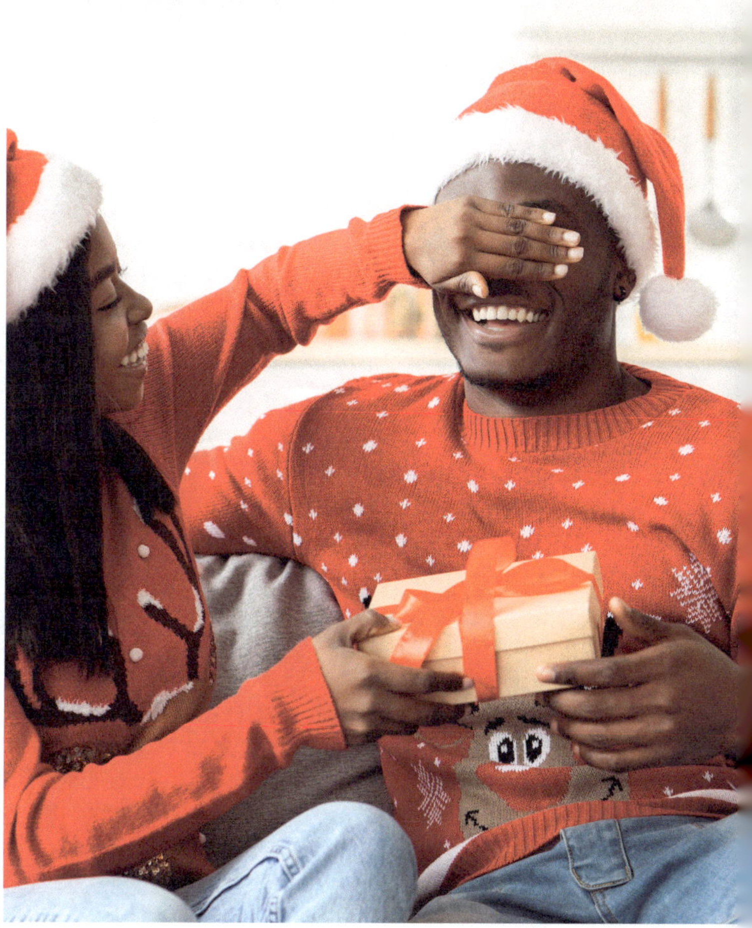
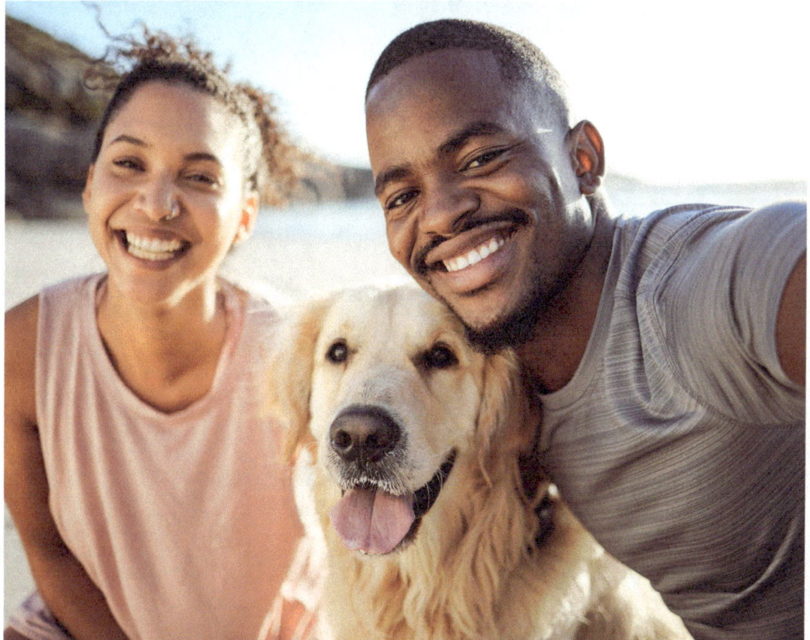
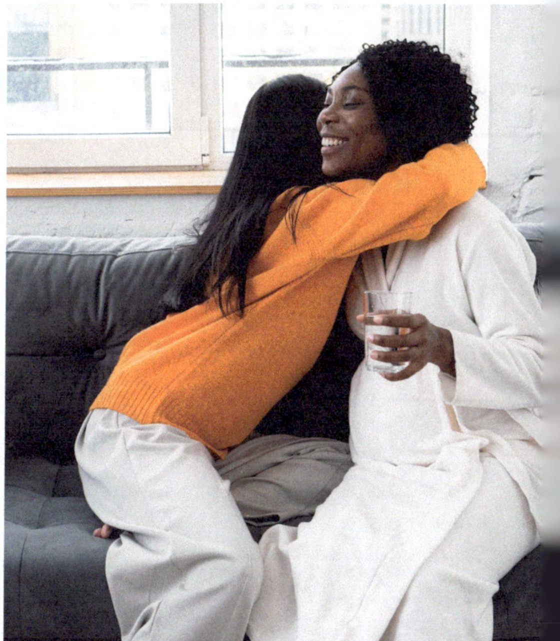

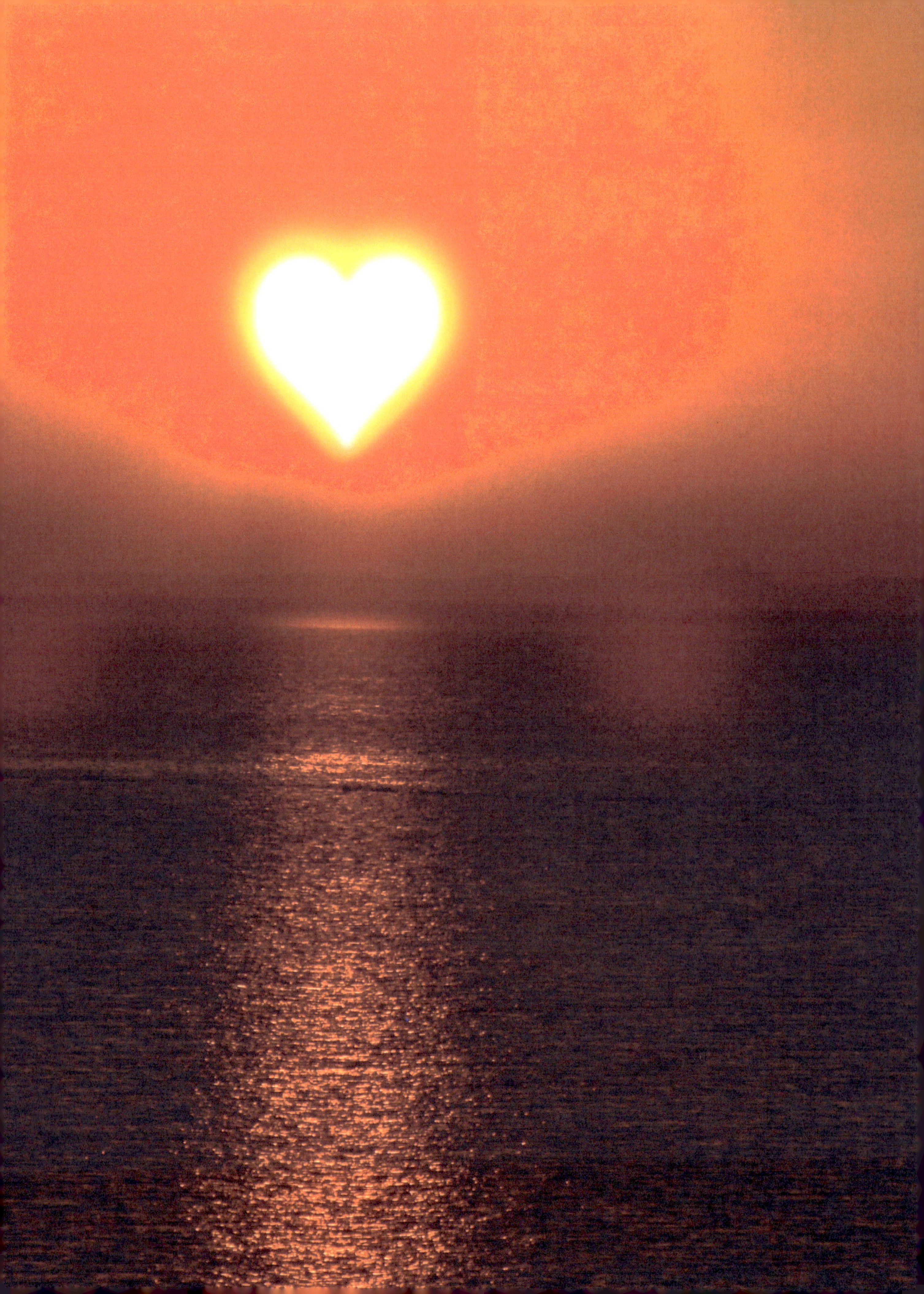

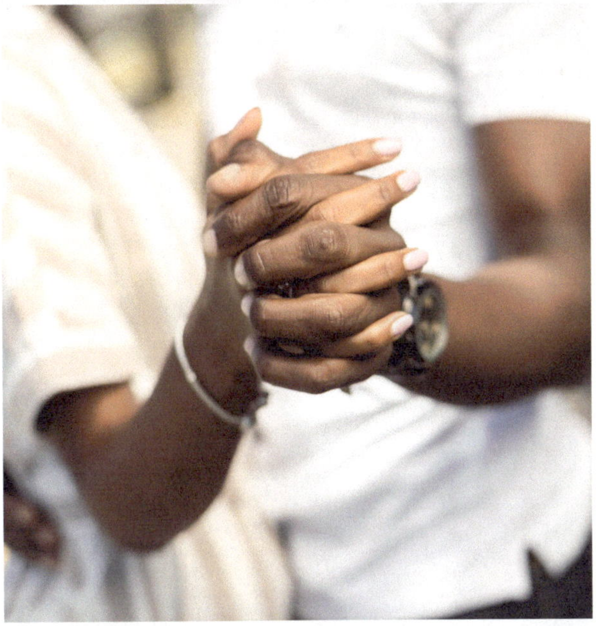
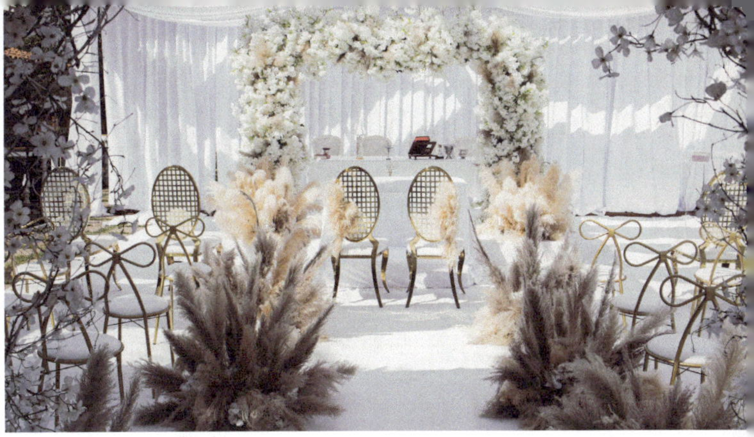
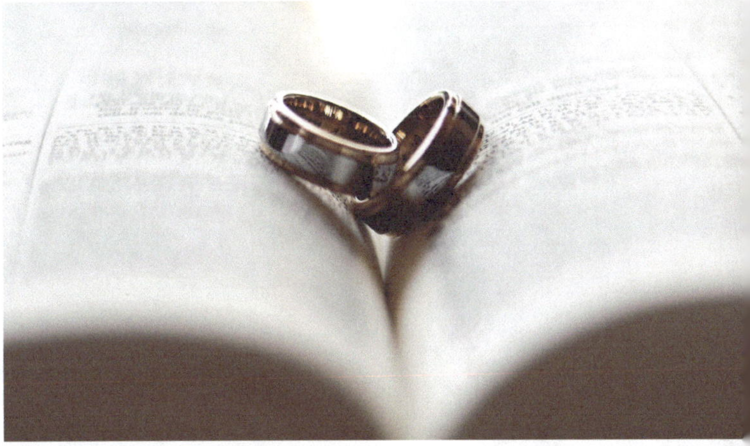
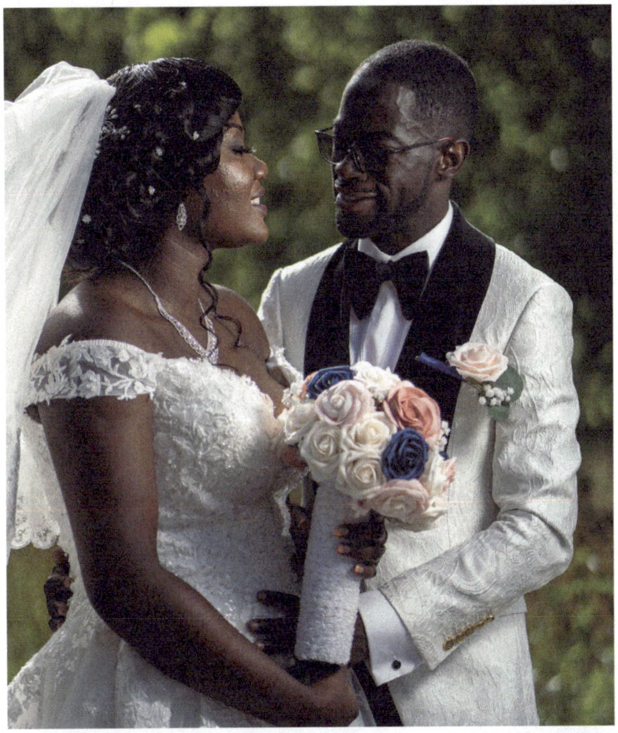
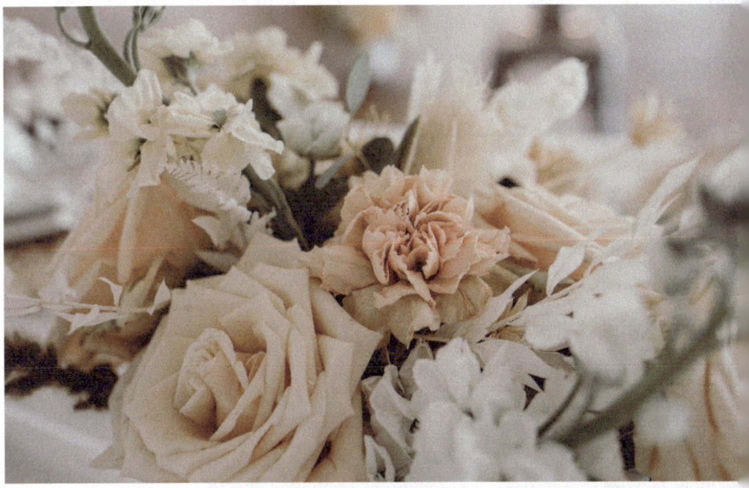
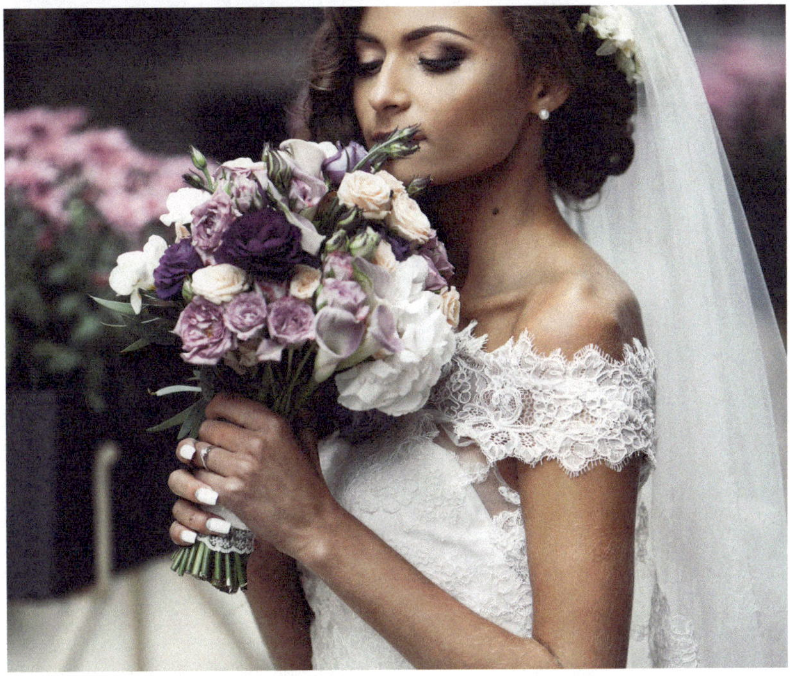

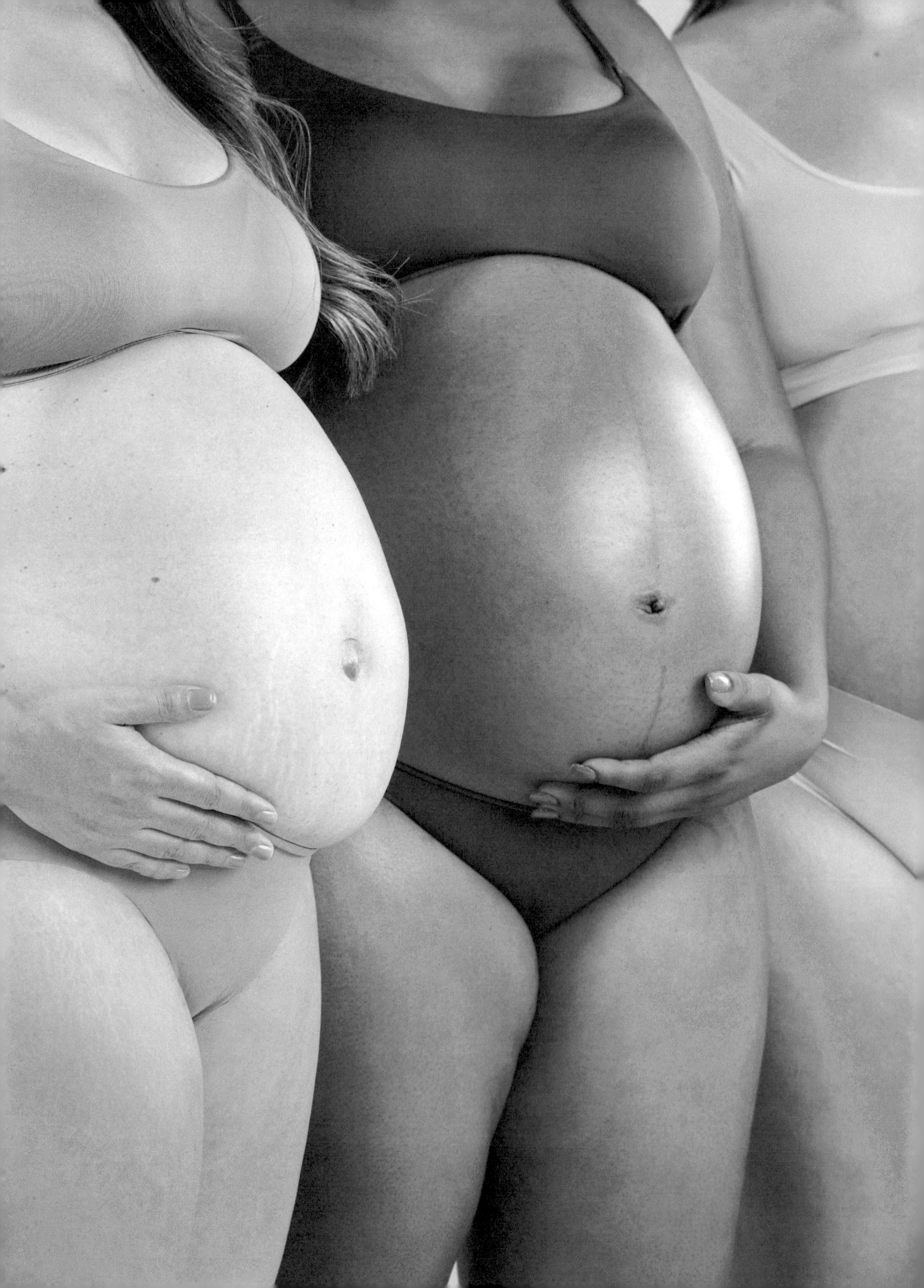

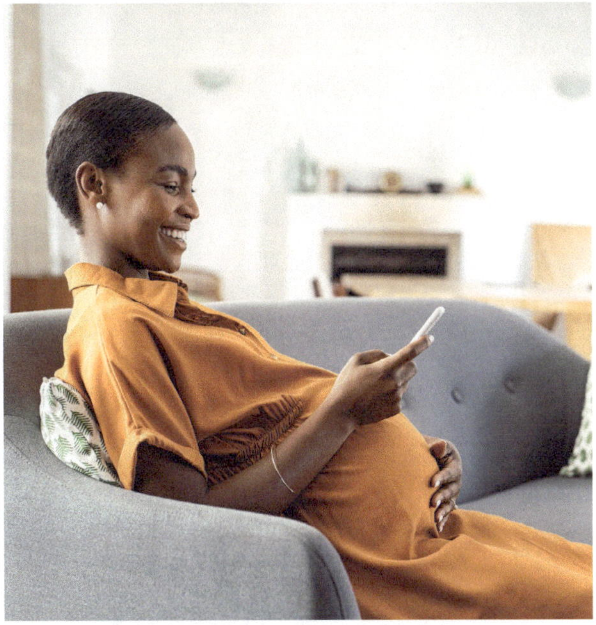
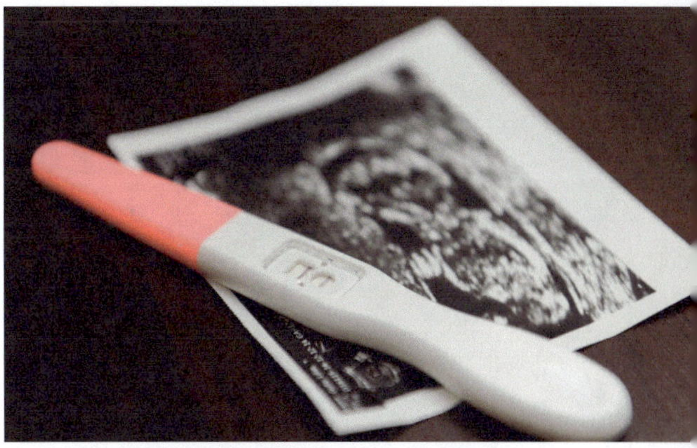
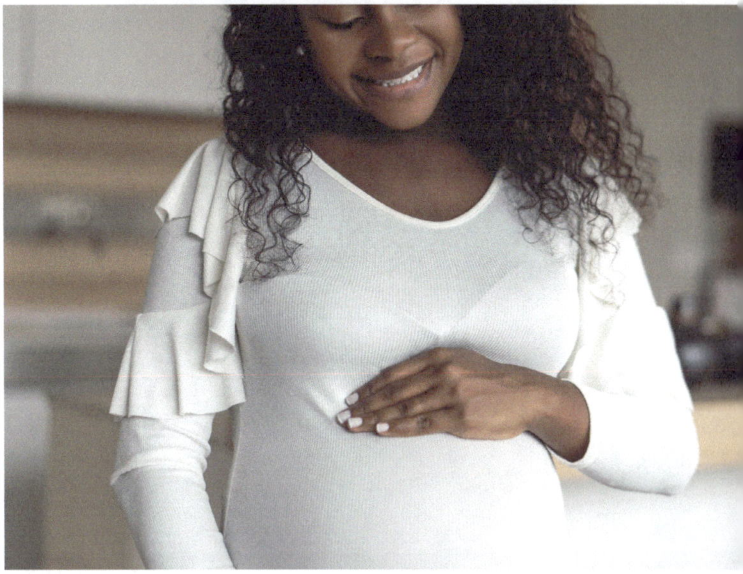
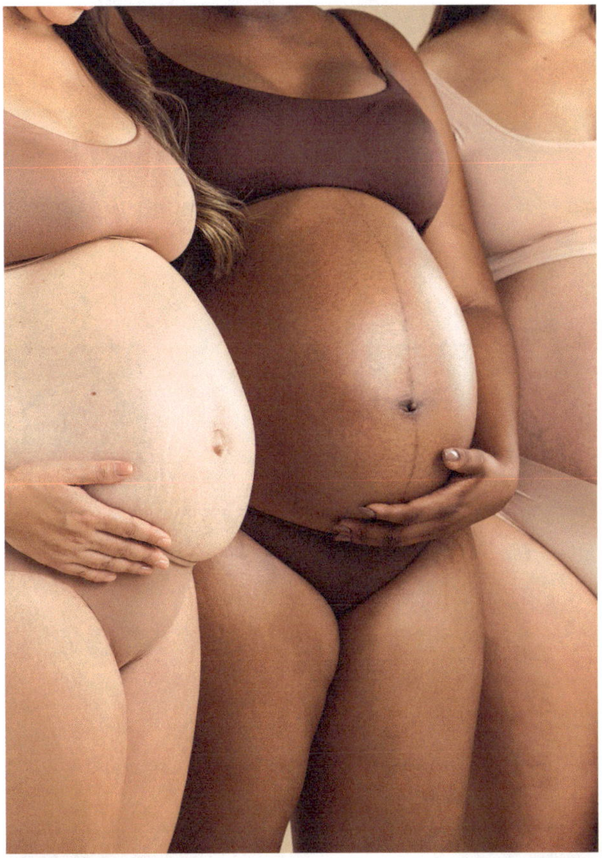
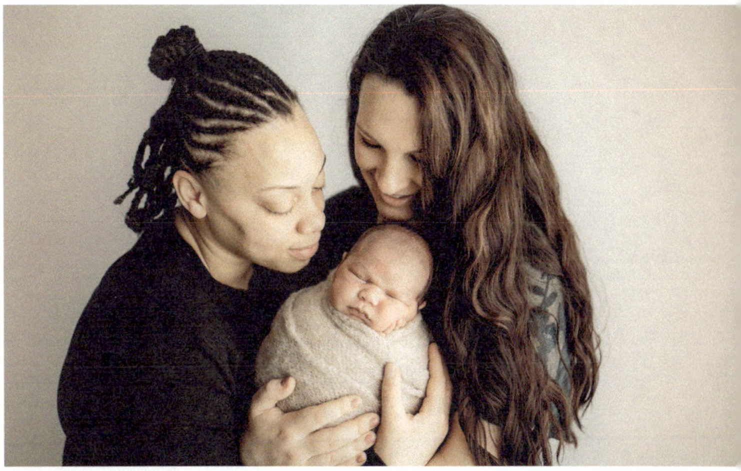
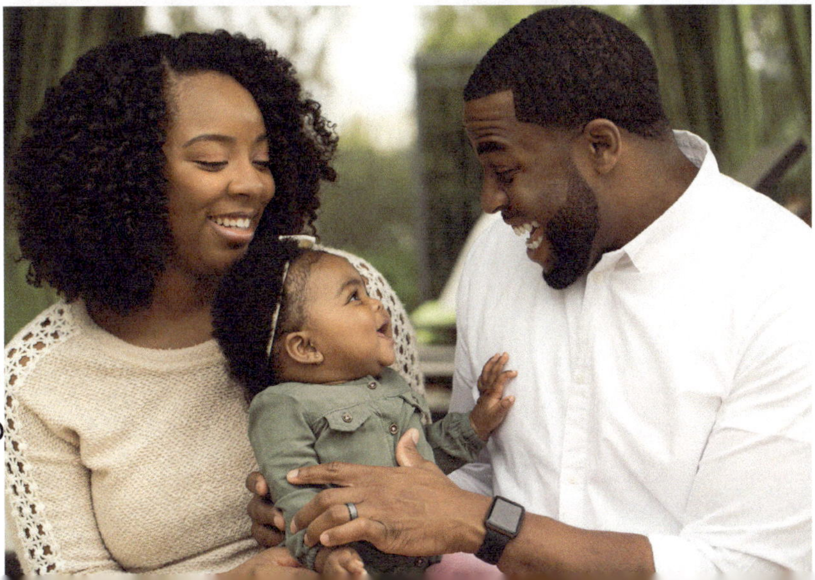
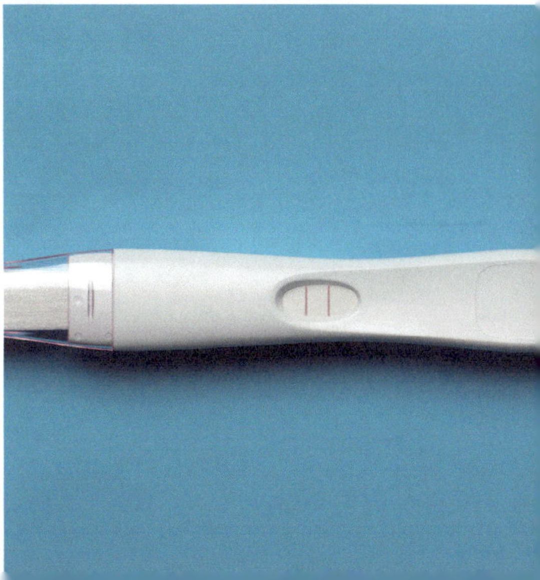

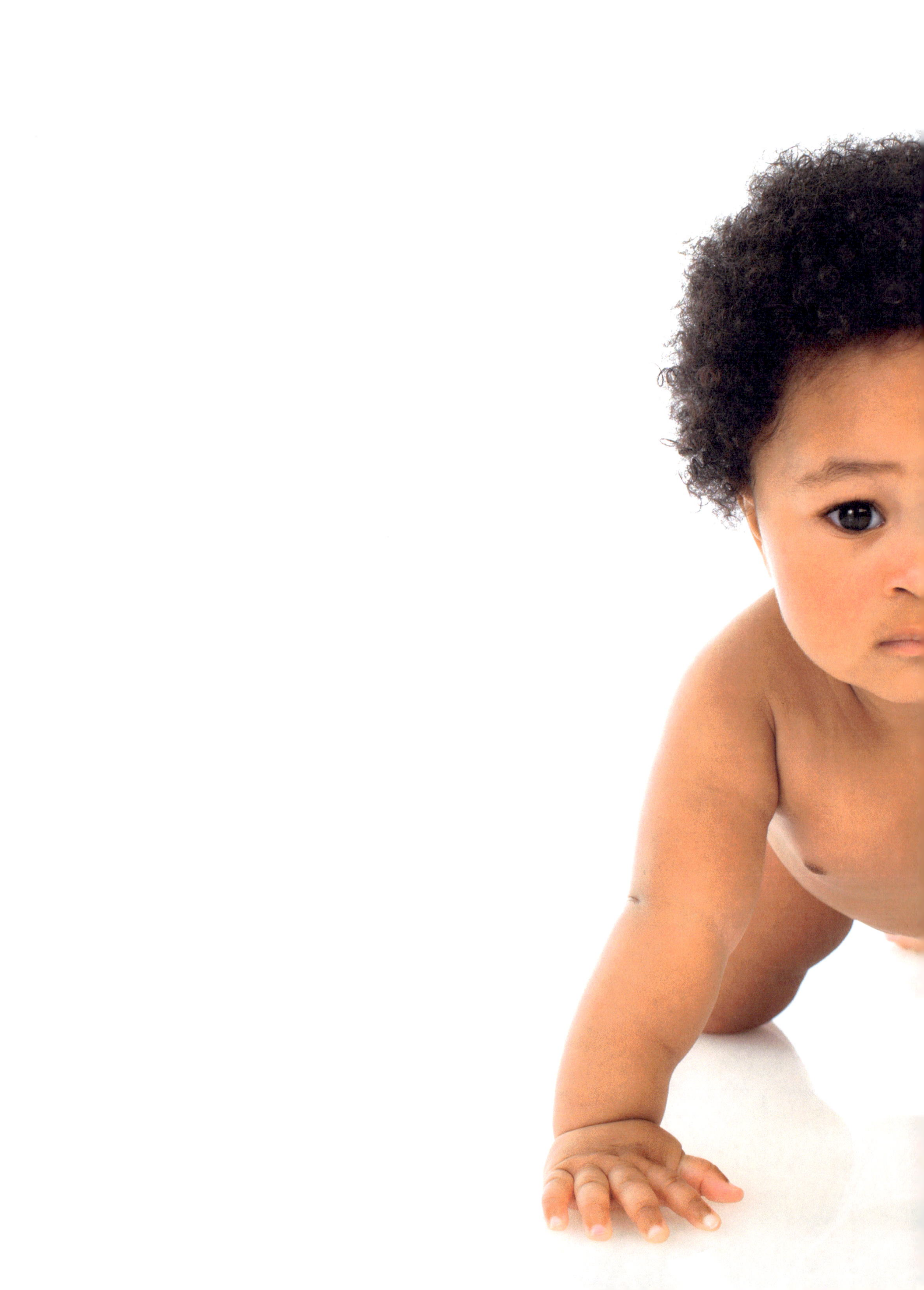

*I am the woman
I want
my daughter
to be*

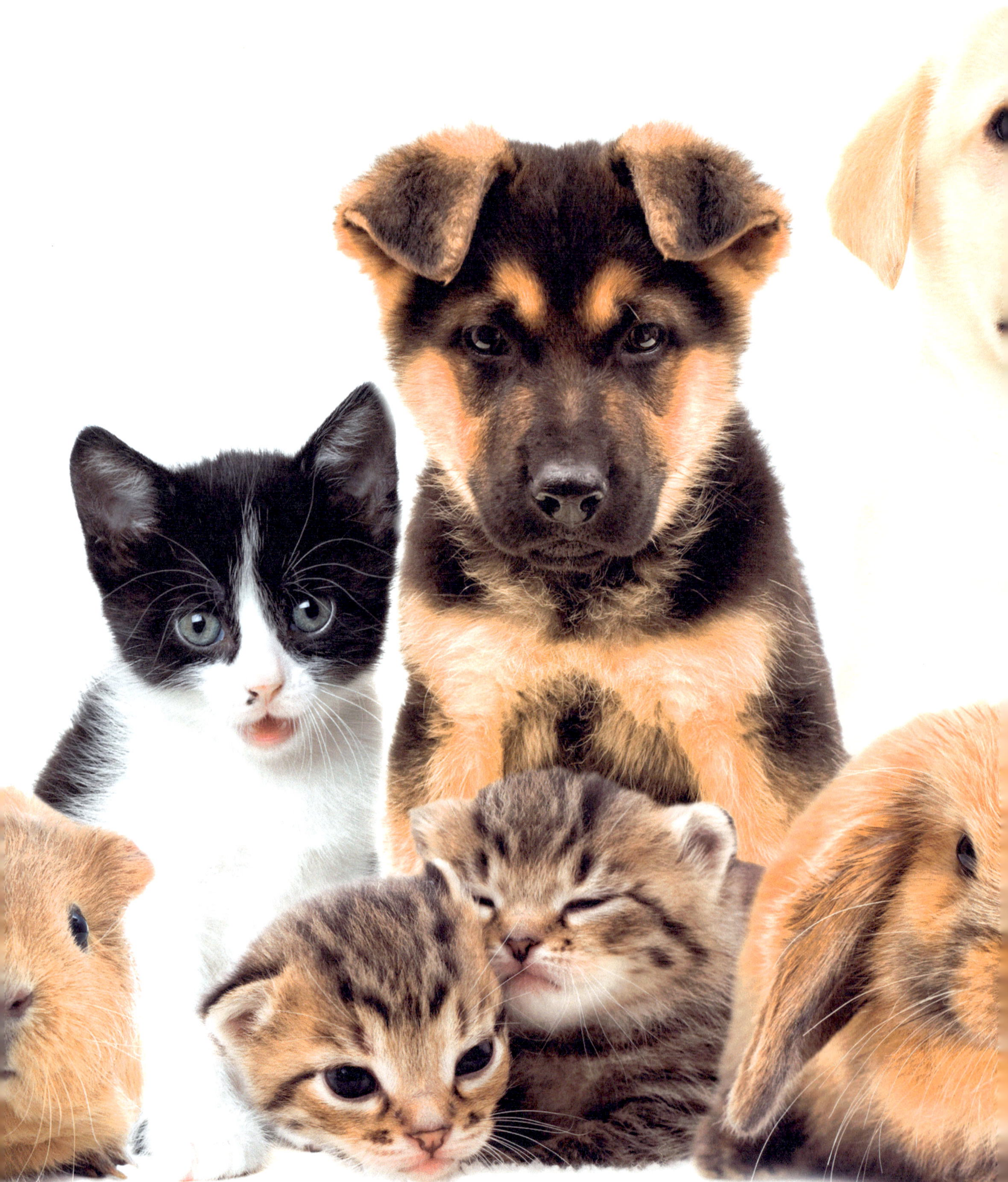

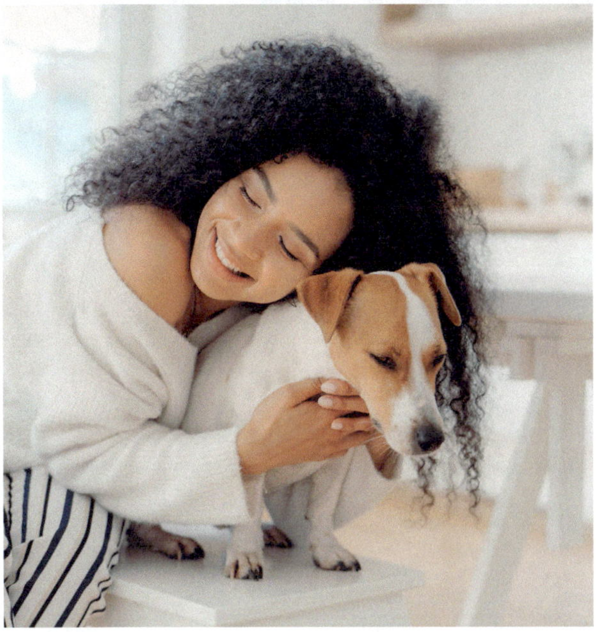
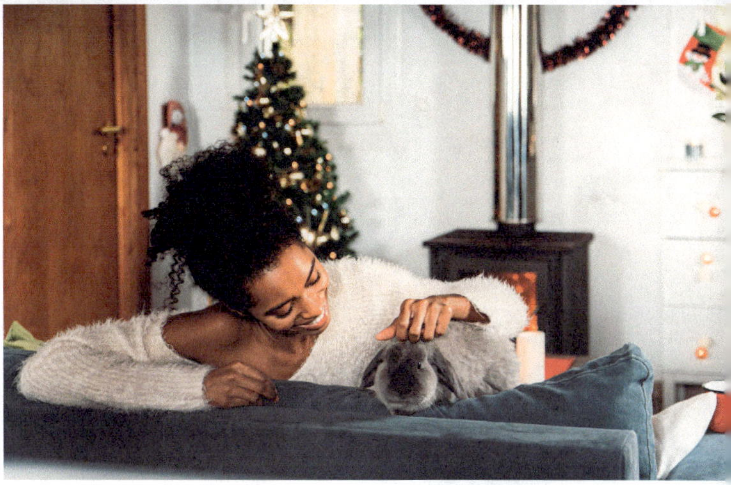
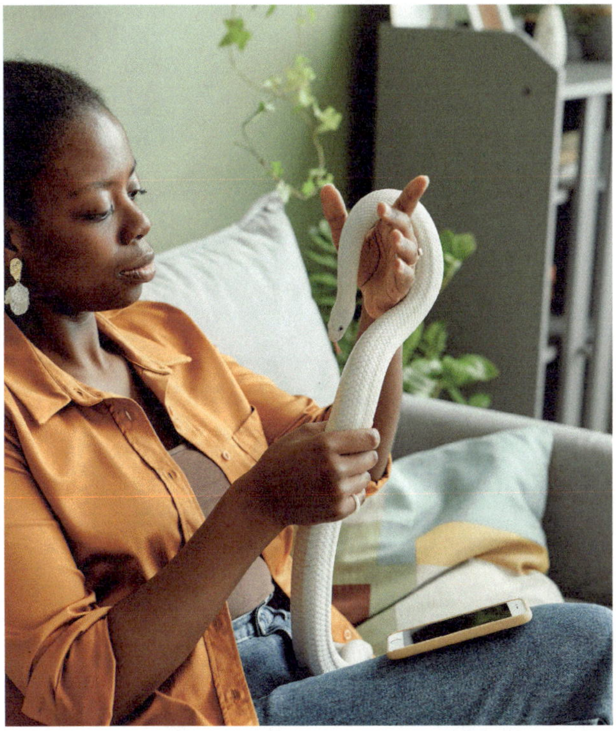
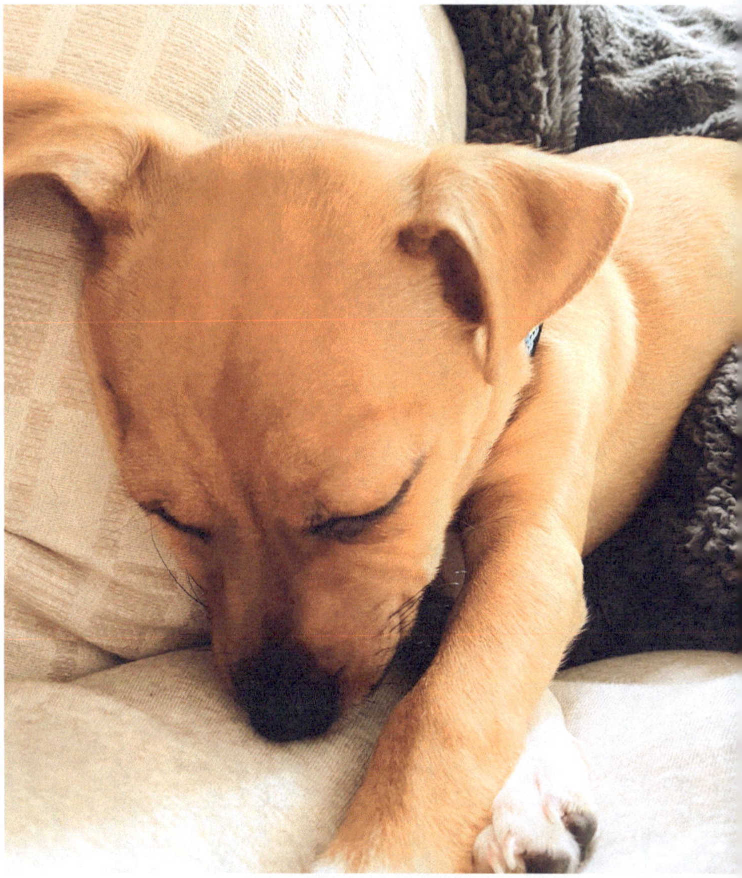
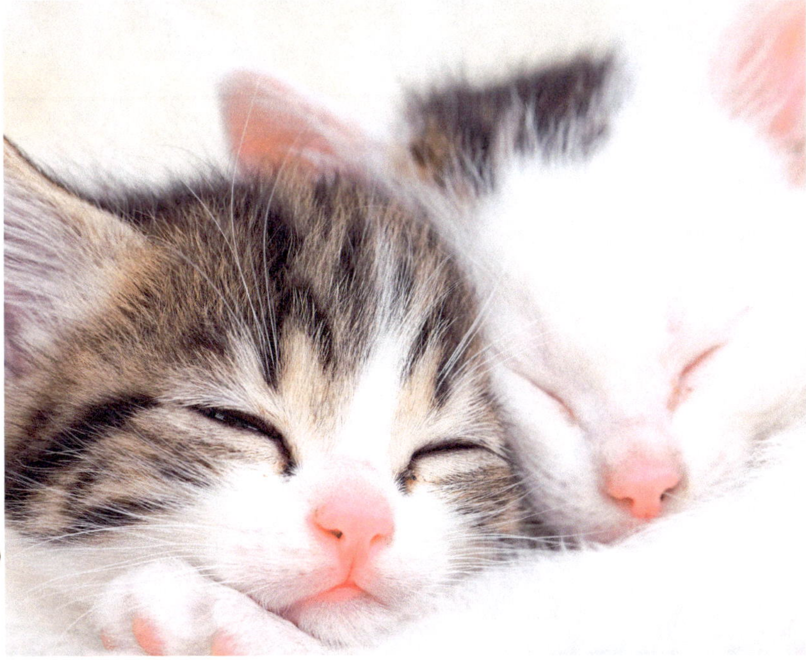
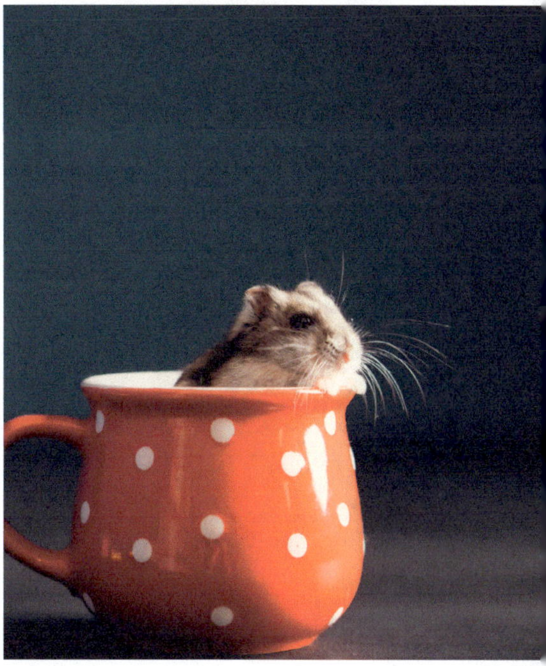

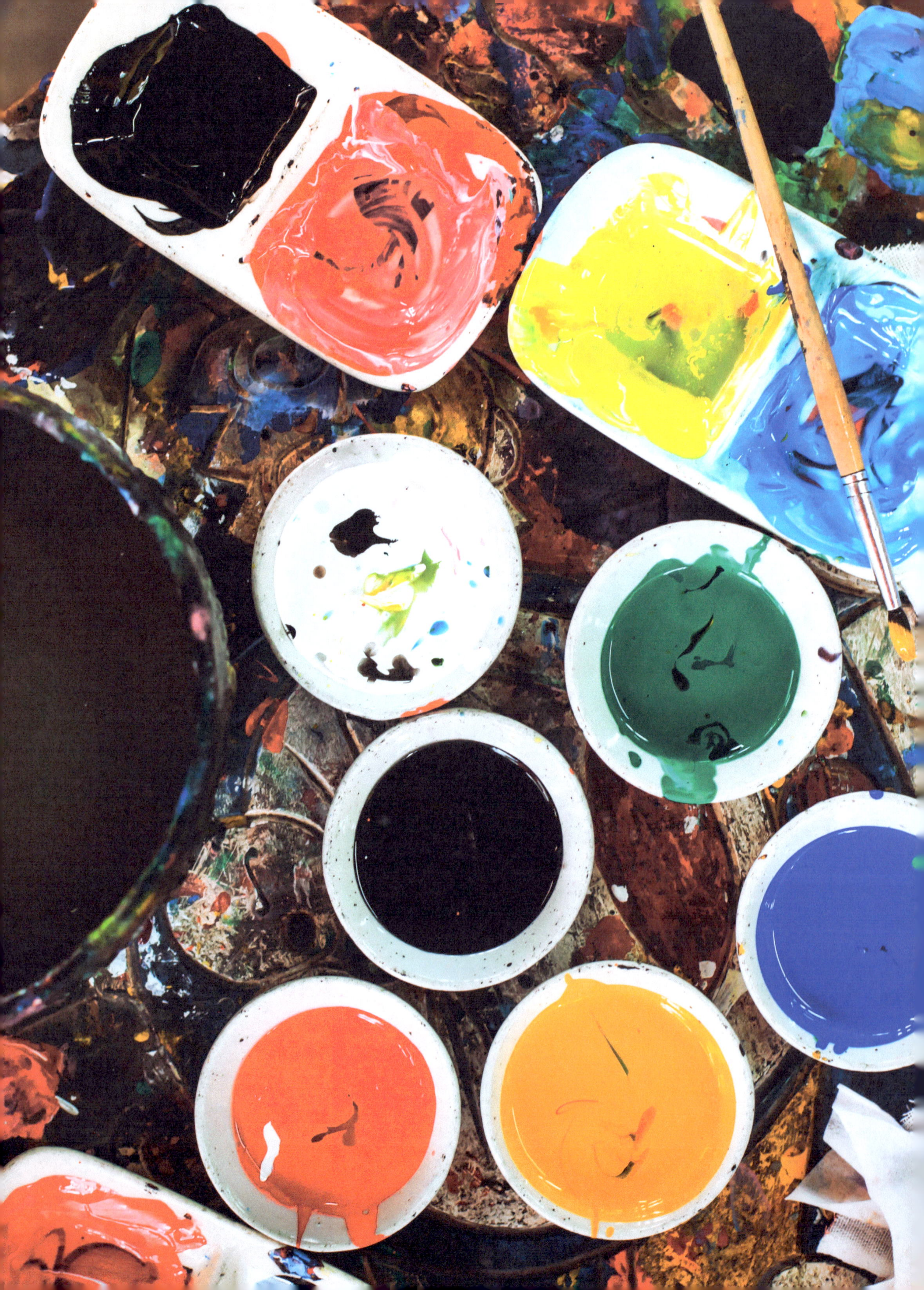

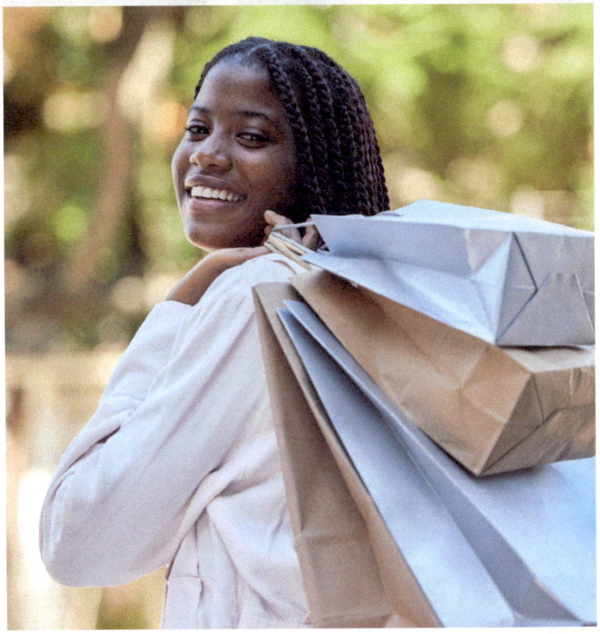
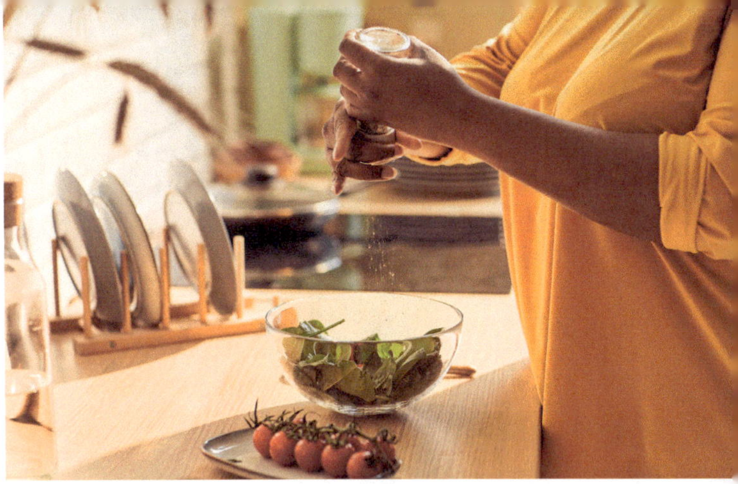
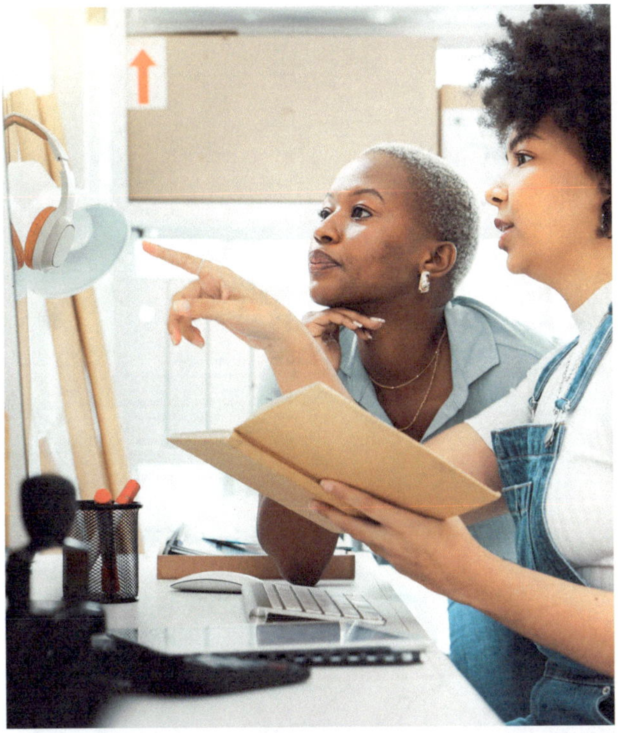
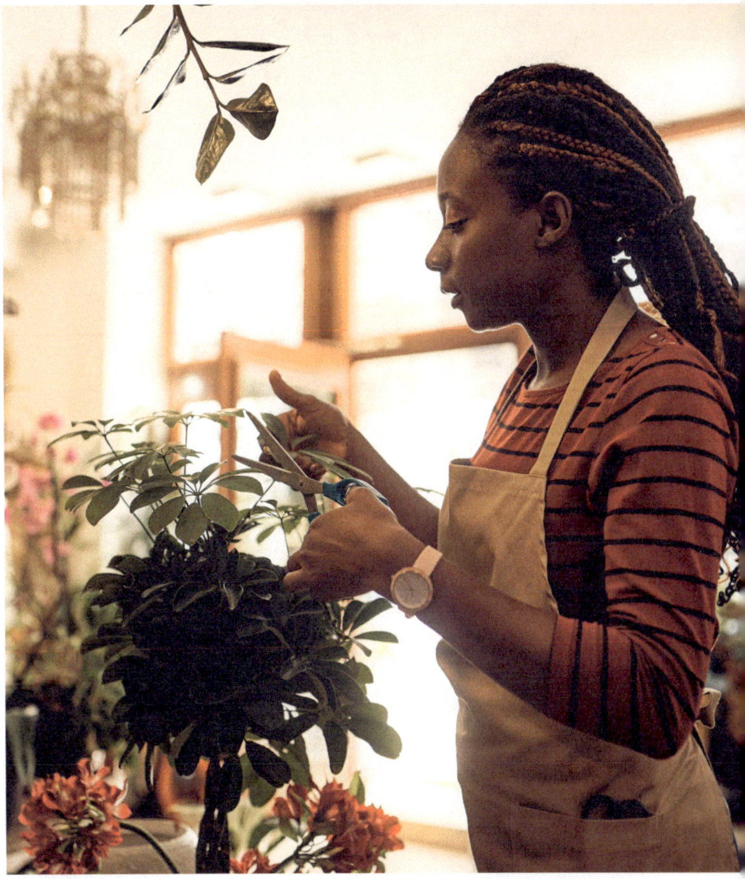
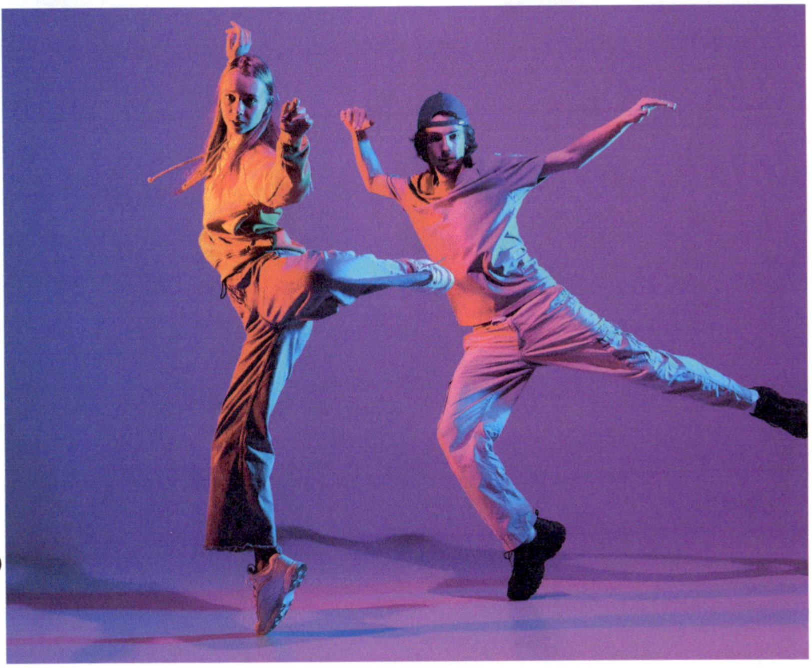
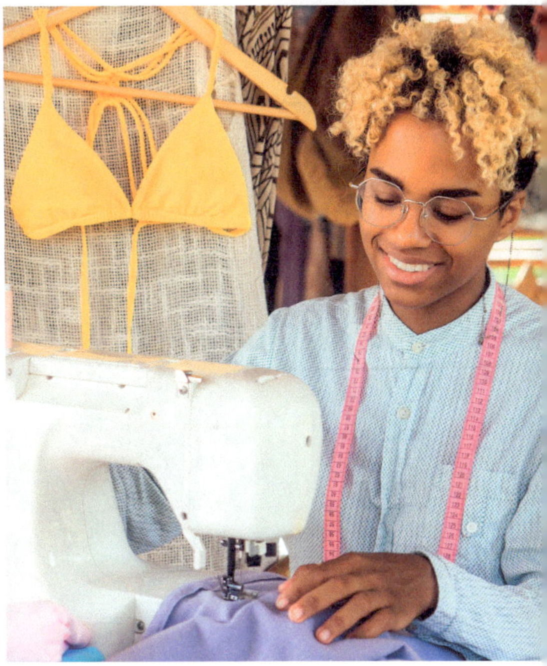

DREAM BIG
SET GOALS
TAKE ACTION

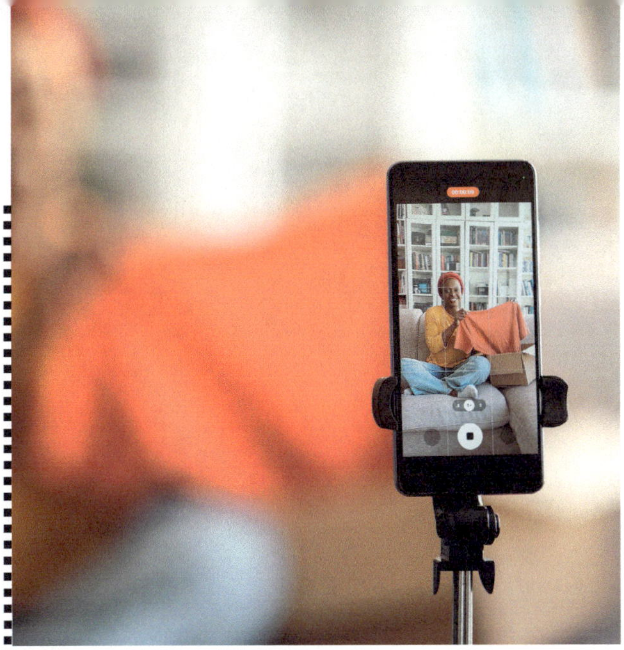
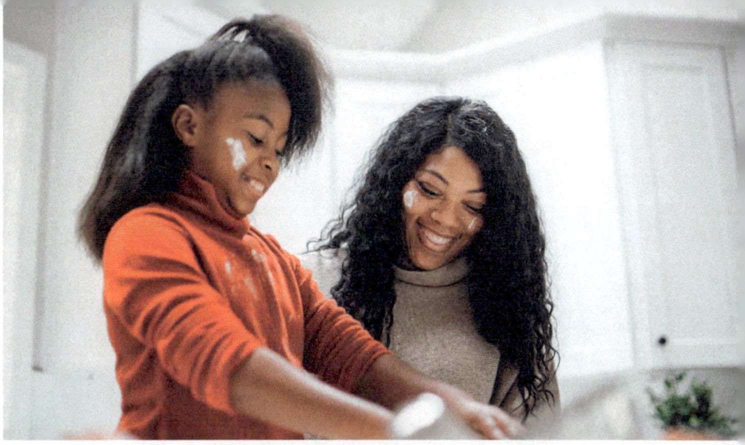
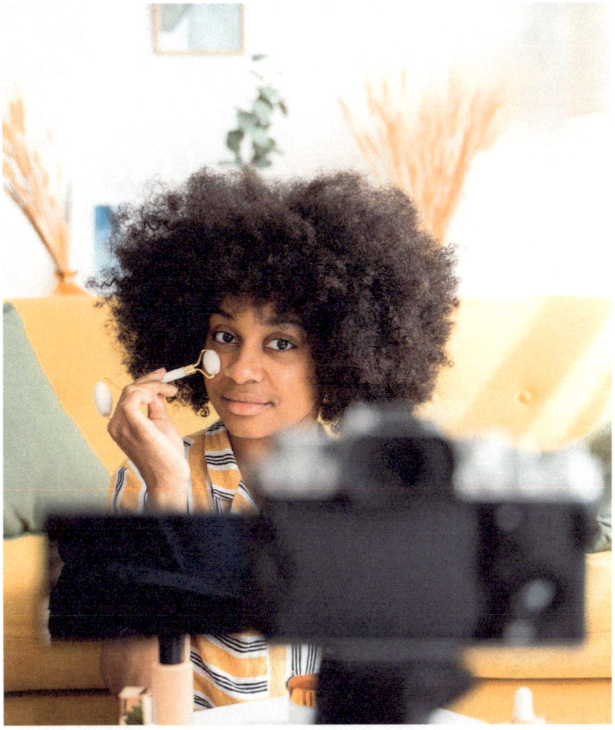
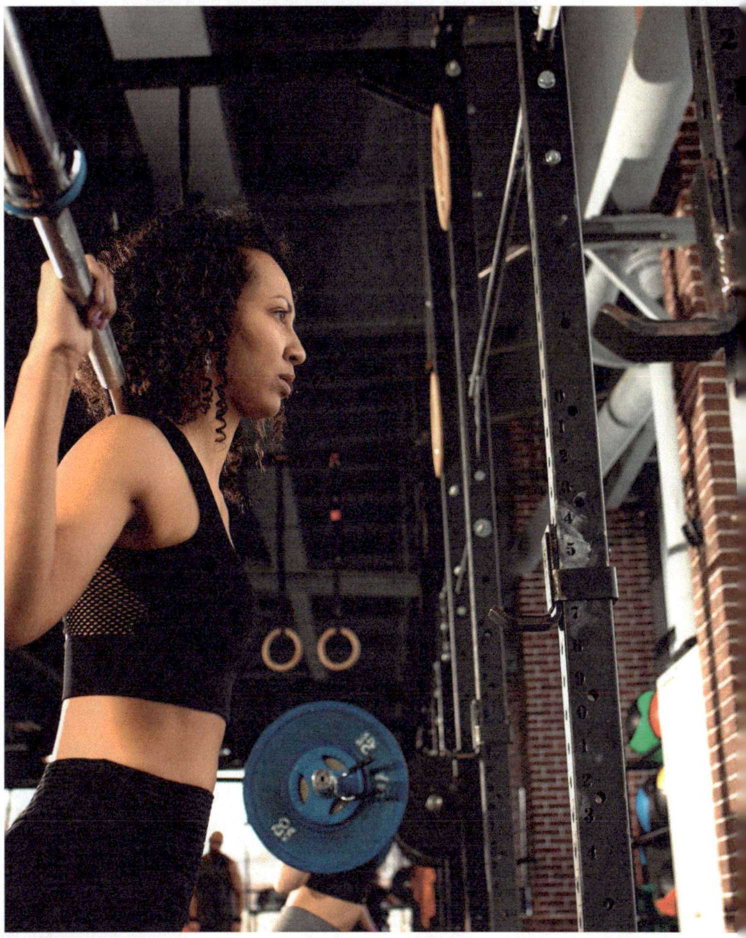
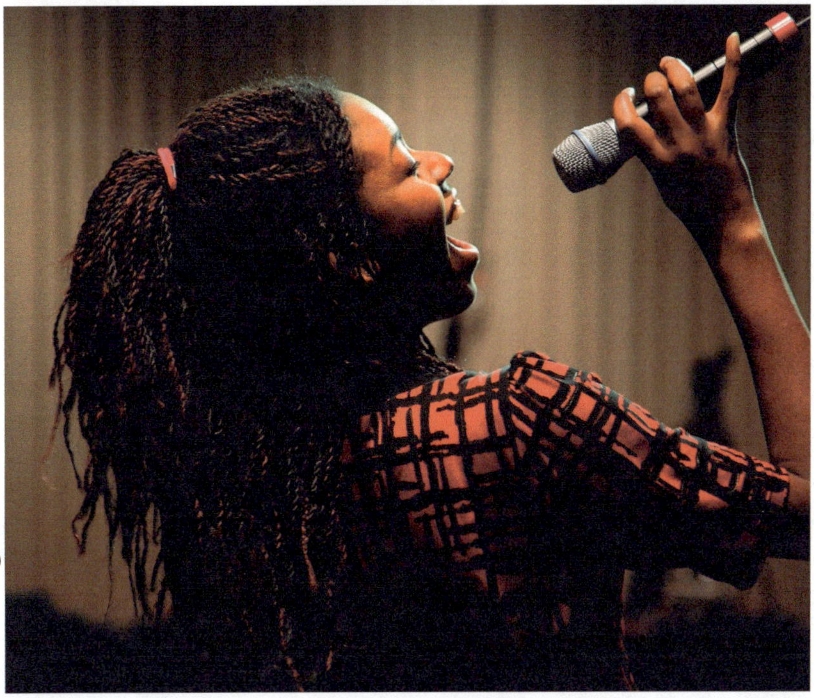
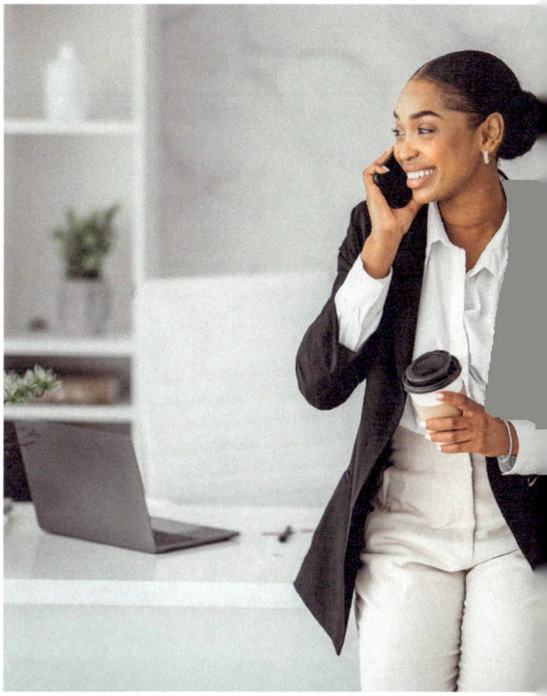

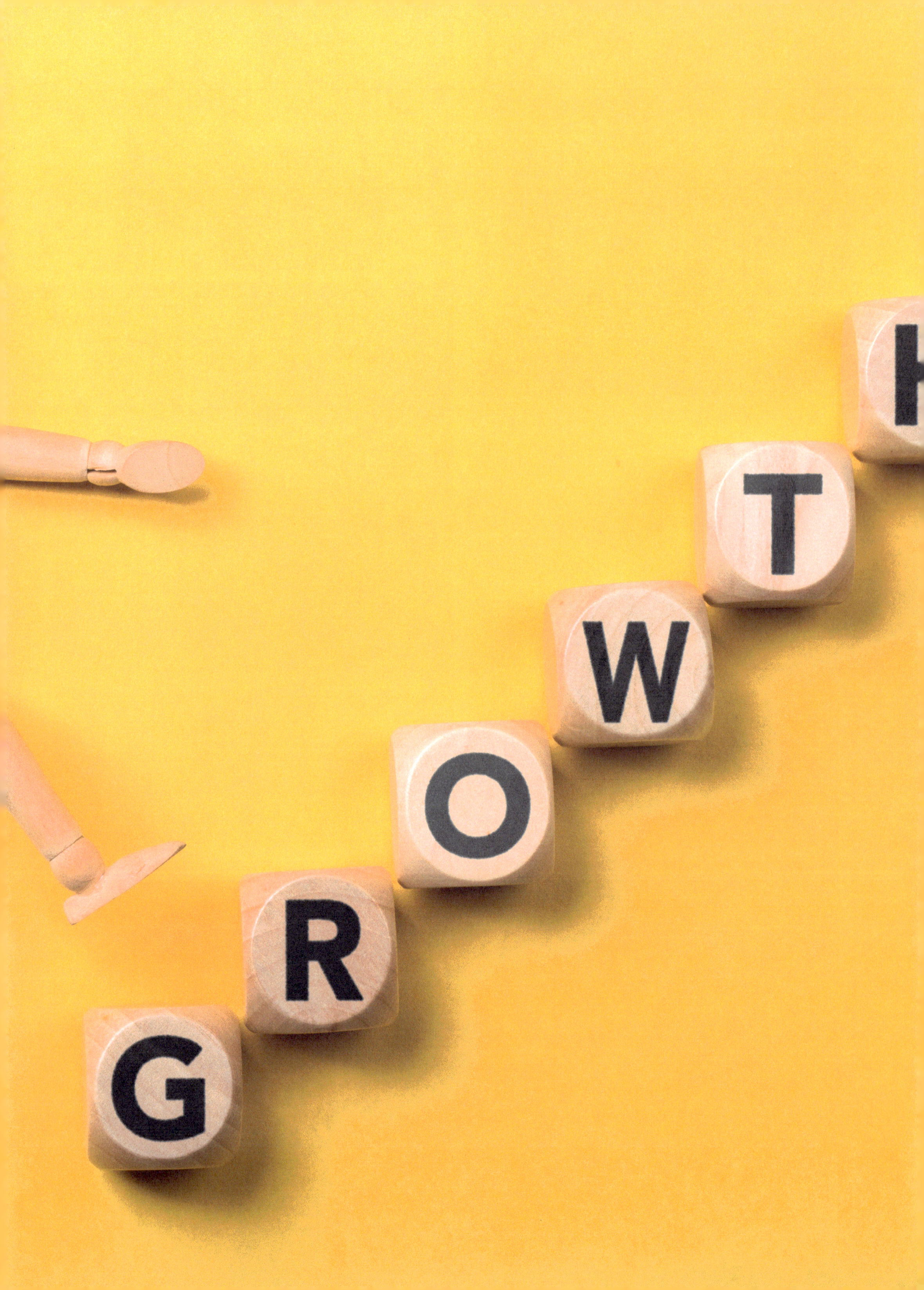
G
R
O
W
T

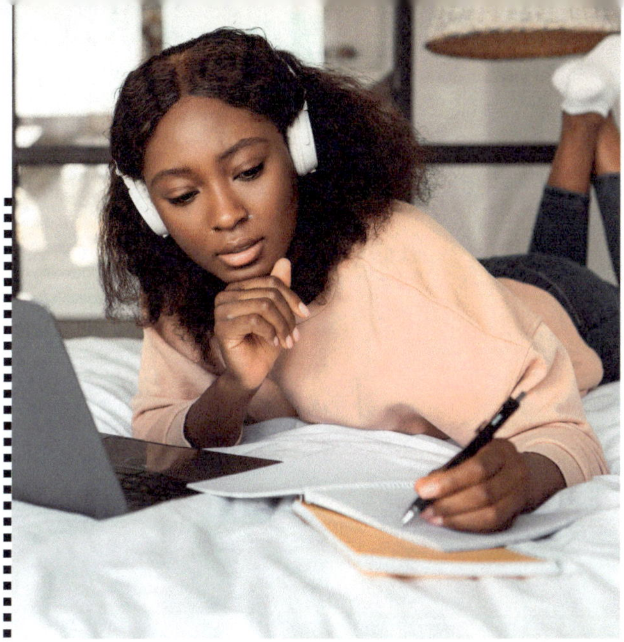

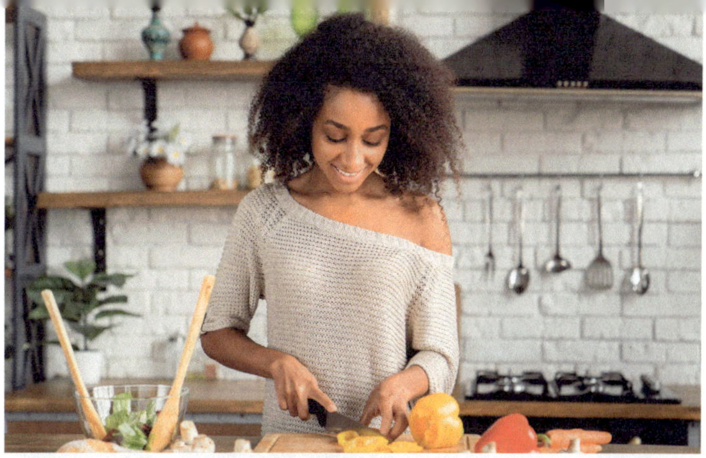

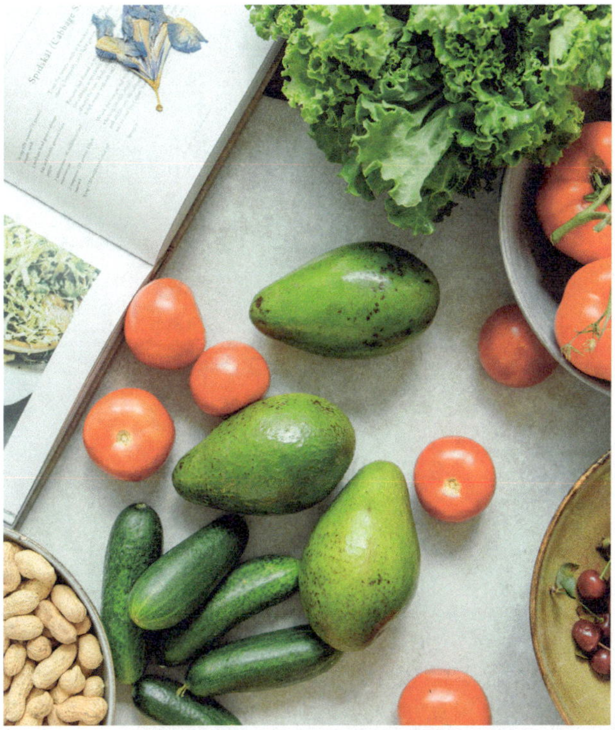

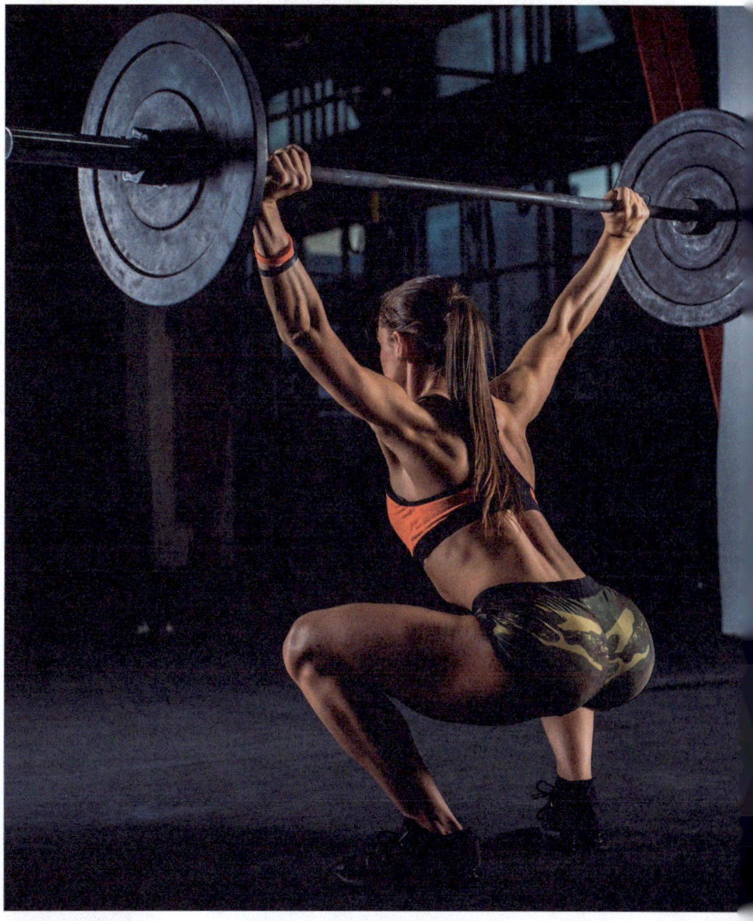

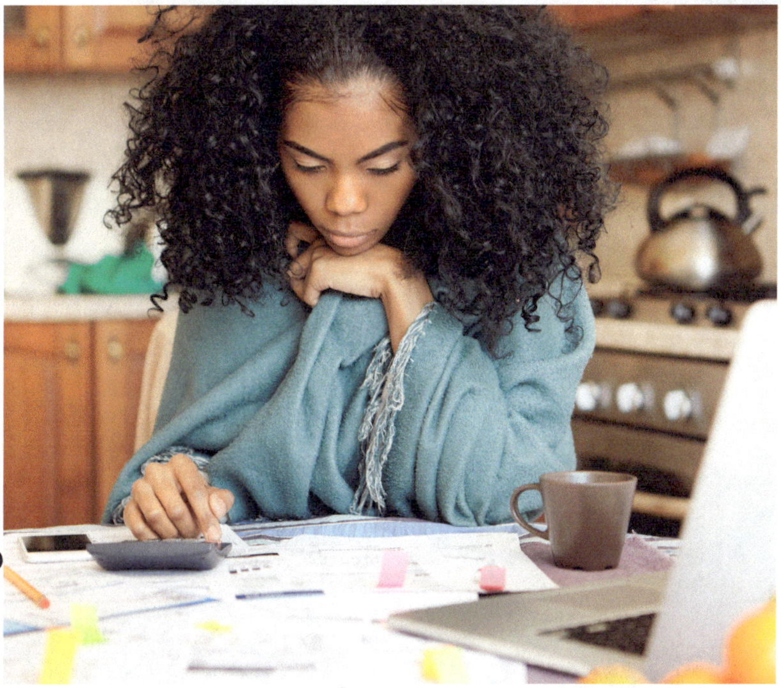

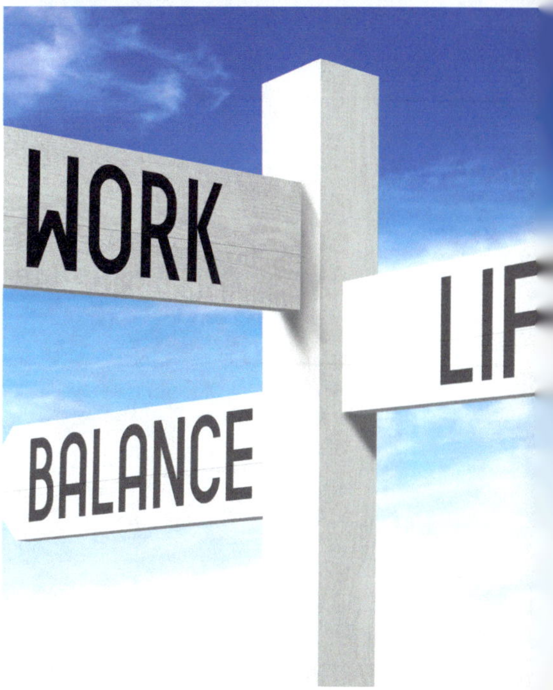
WORK
BALANCE

01010101010101 deconi human
Global_Tech

command creation mode path
retina path 01HG Deoded error

RESULT
01010101010101 deconi human
Global_Tech
command creation mode path retina path 01HG

MVK PRO0111
command creation mode path
retina path 01HG Deoded error

01/
01010101010101 deconi human
Global_Tech
command creation mode path retina path 01HG

45.02
command creation mode path
retina path 01HG Deoded error

01010101010101 deconig
human Global_Tech
command
maode path 1010HER
Deoded error

010
Global
command
retina path

0101010
Global

GOAL

Relate & Radiate

"Deal with yourself as an individual worthy of respect, and make everyone else deal with you the same way." - Nikki Giovanni.

How does the way you treat yourself set the standard for how others treat you, and what steps can you take to strengthen this self-respect in your relationships?

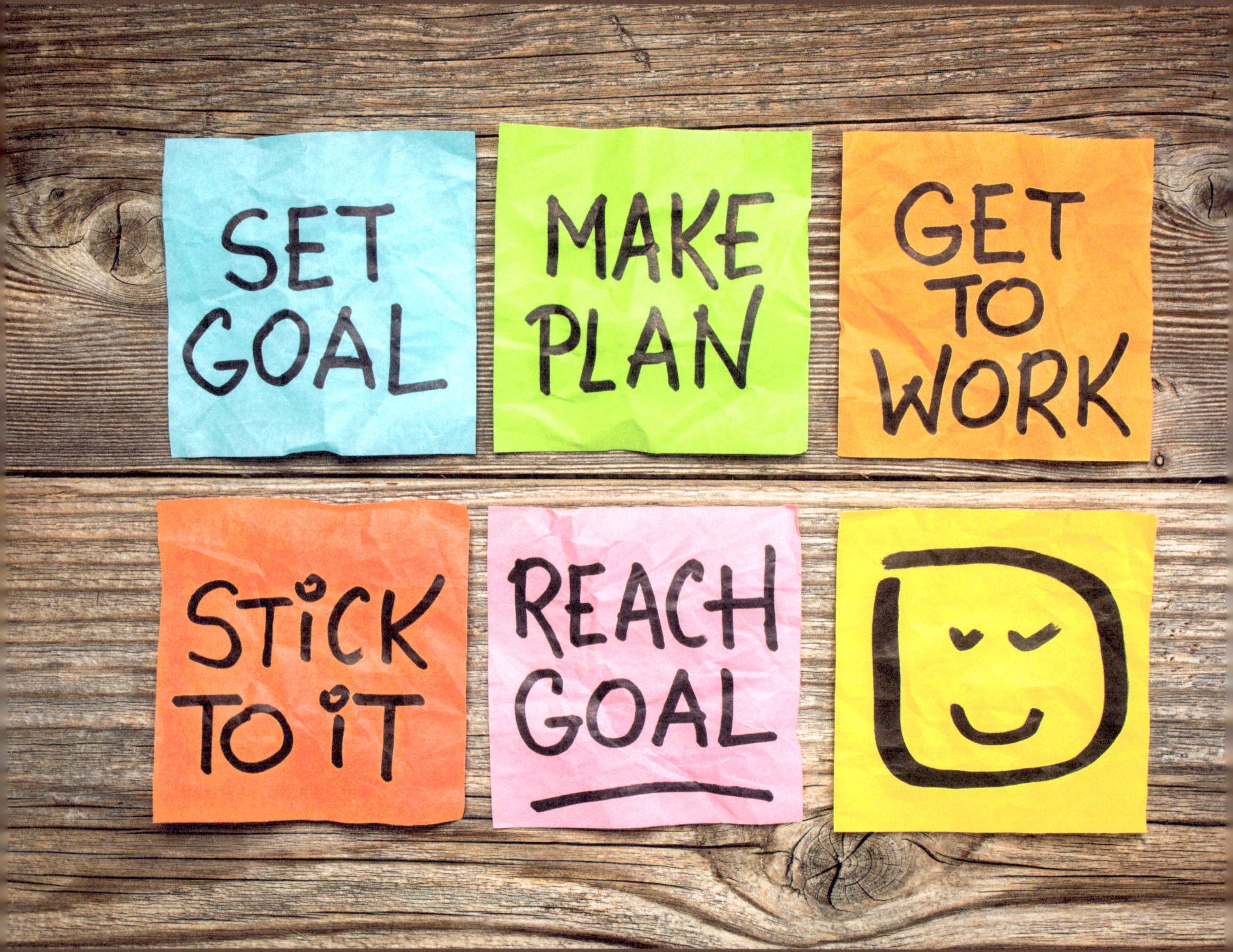
SET GOAL
MAKE PLAN
GET TO WORK
STICK TO IT
REACH GOAL

Pay day

FINANCIAL control

MONEY management

CROWD funding

INVESTMENT strategy

revenue

PLAN BUDGET	BUDGET	EXPENSES
SALARY	UPDATE EXPENSES	RATES
MORTGAGE	RENT	HOUSING

CALL doctor

VISIT dentist

EYE clinic

mental health break

PHYSICAL therapy

TAKE medicines

appointment

appointment

medicine
M T W T F S

| DR.APPOINTMENT | DENTIST APPOINTMENT | PRESCRIPTION |
| FITNESS | SELF CARE | INSURANCE |

FORGIVE

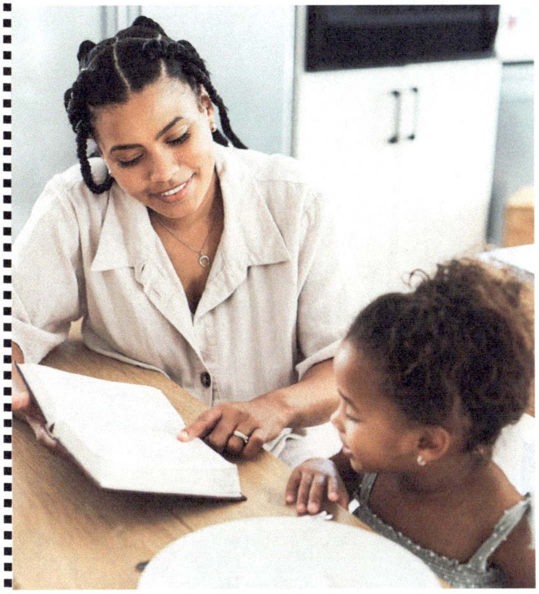
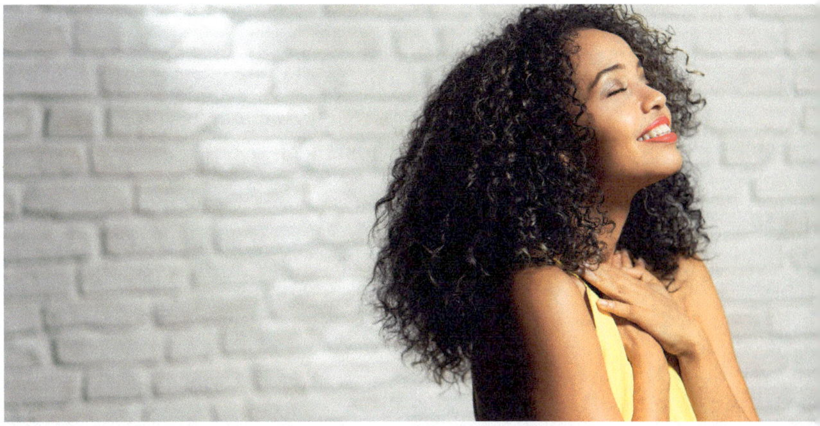
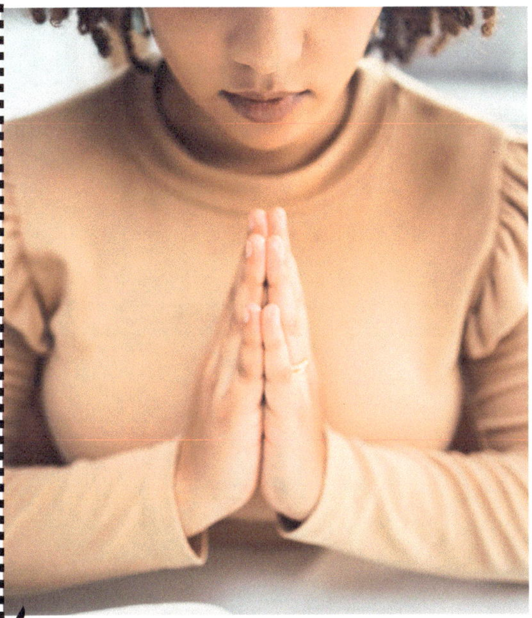
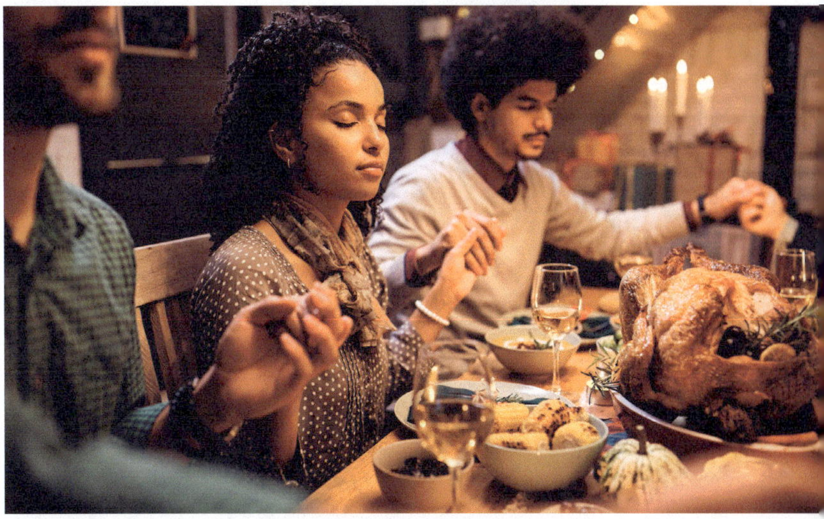
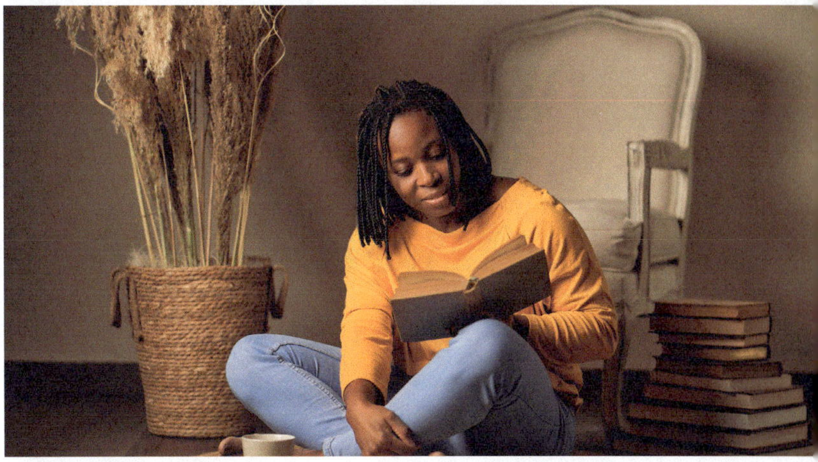
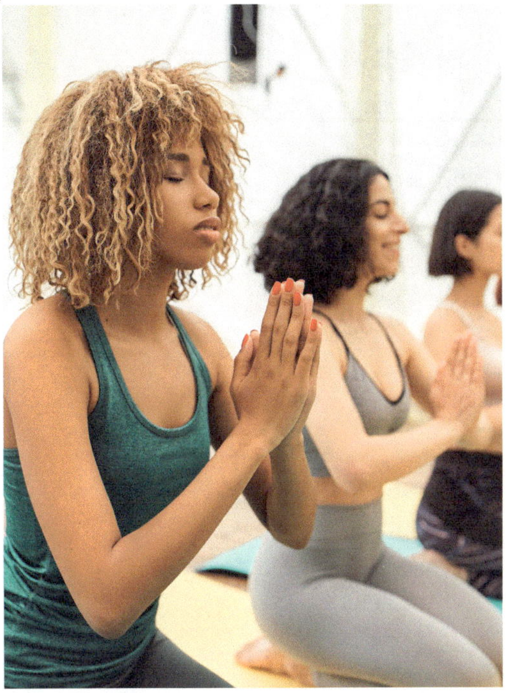
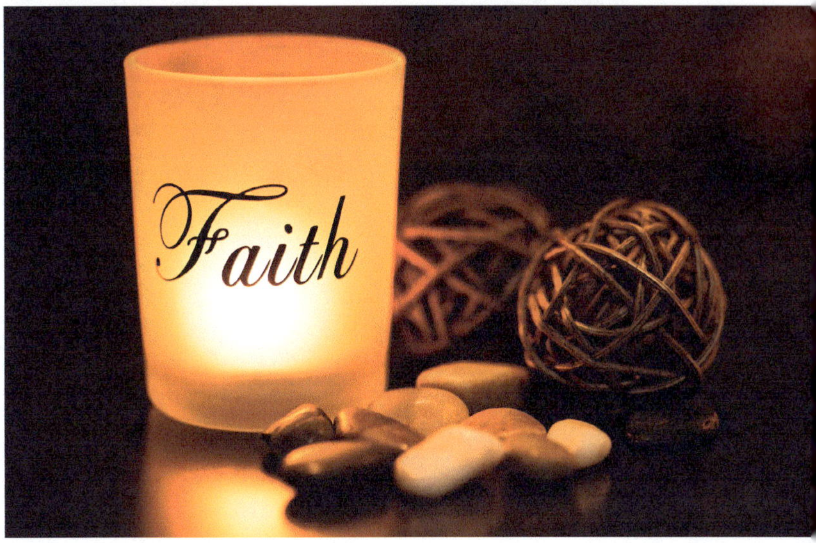
Faith

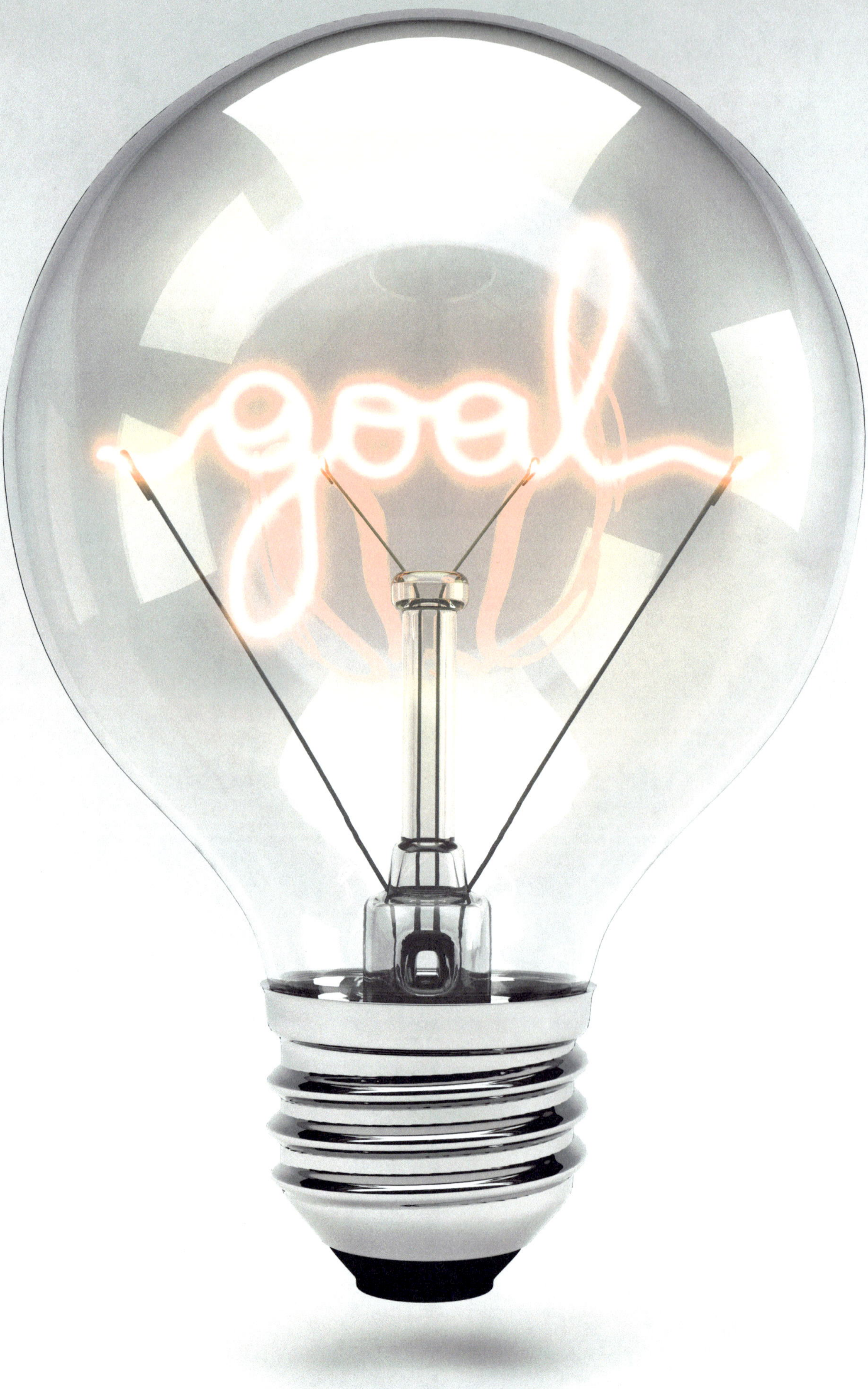
goal

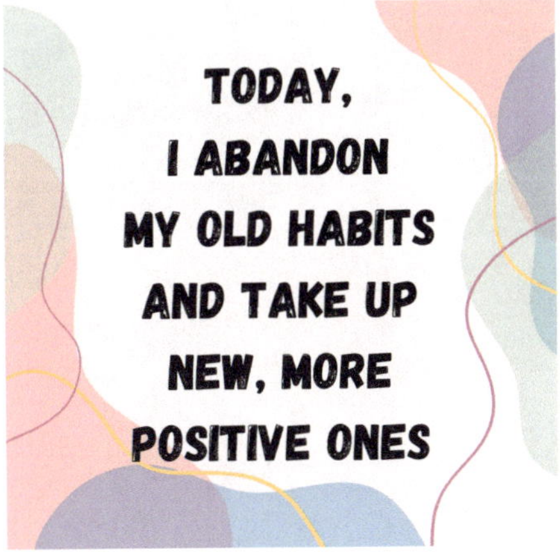

TODAY, I ABANDON MY OLD HABITS AND TAKE UP NEW, MORE POSITIVE ONES	 GIRL BOSS	 Embrace your culture, for it is the melody that dances in your soul and the unique story of who you are
 I RADIATE CONFIDENCE AND GRACE IN EVERY STEP I TAKE	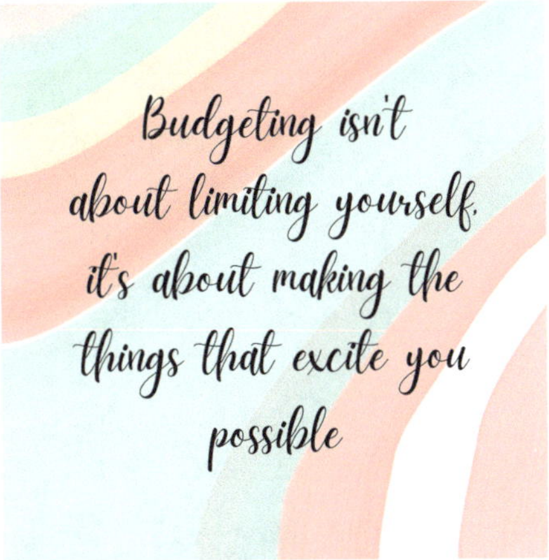 Budgeting isn't about limiting yourself, it's about making the things that excite you possible	 Financial freedom is more than having money — it's the liberation to live life on your own terms.
 TRUE LOVE IS LIKE A FINE WINE, IT GETS BETTER WITH TIME, DEEPENING IN FLAVOR AND VALUE	 I am courageous and stand up for myself	 MY FAITH IS LARGER THAN MY FEARS, AND MY DREAMS LARGER THAN MY DOUBTS
 I will not compare myself to strangers on the Internet	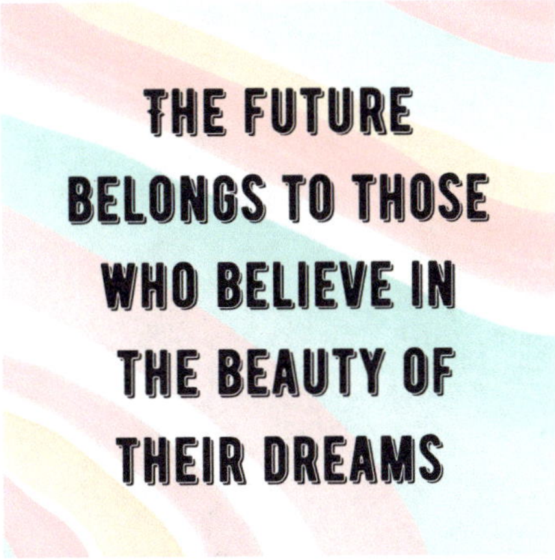 THE FUTURE BELONGS TO THOSE WHO BELIEVE IN THE BEAUTY OF THEIR DREAMS	 Keeping my STANDARDS and HEELS HIGH. You couldn't handle me if you had INSTRUCTIONS

YOUR HABITS

DECIDE

YOUR FUTURE

A GOAL IS A DREAM WITH A DEADLINE

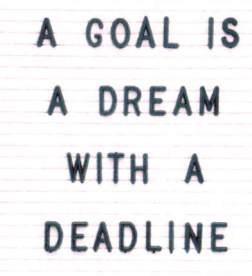

MORE SOCIAL LESS MEDIA

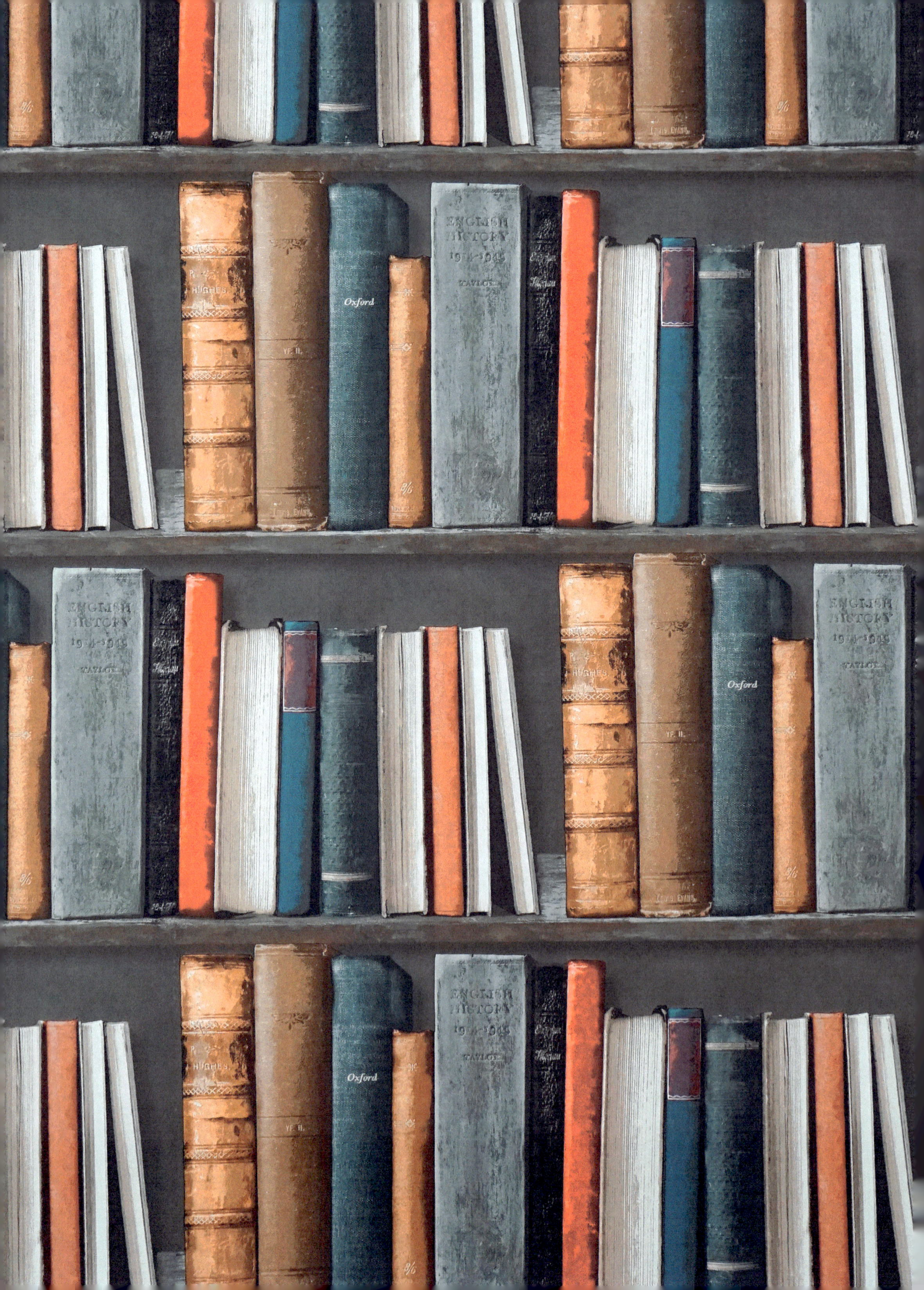
ENGLISH HISTORY
Oxford

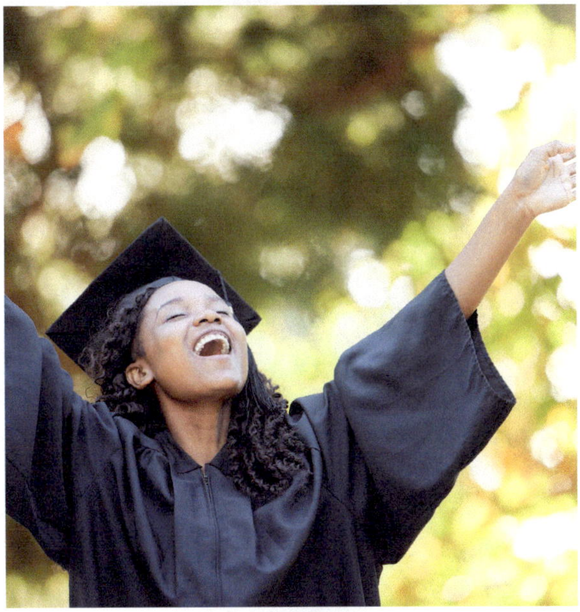
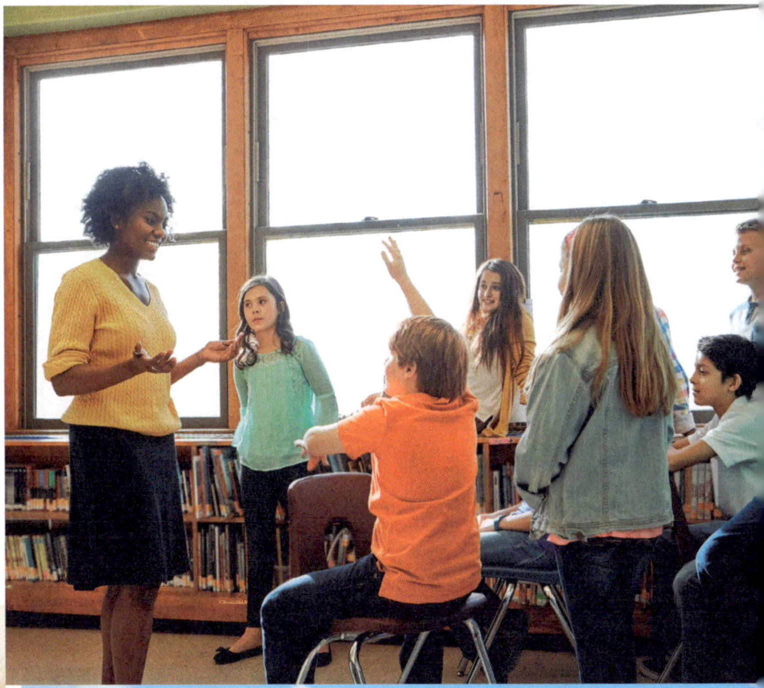
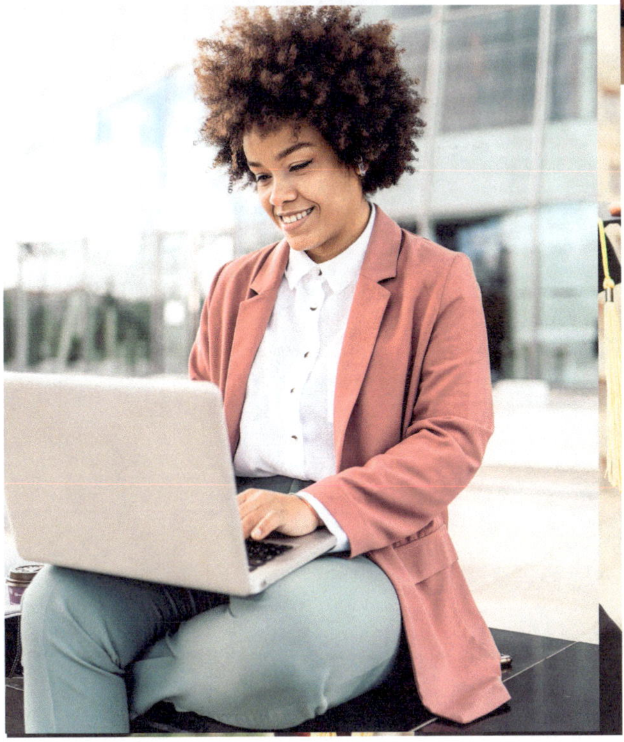
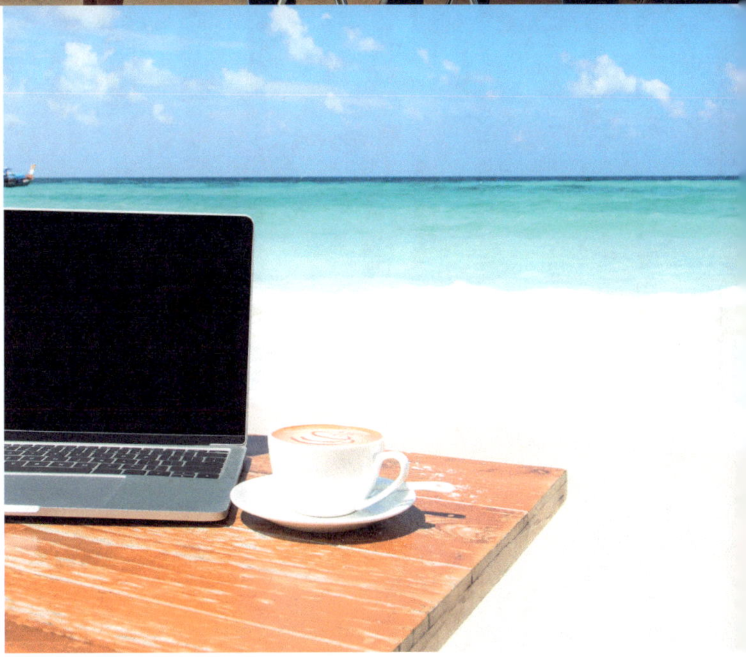
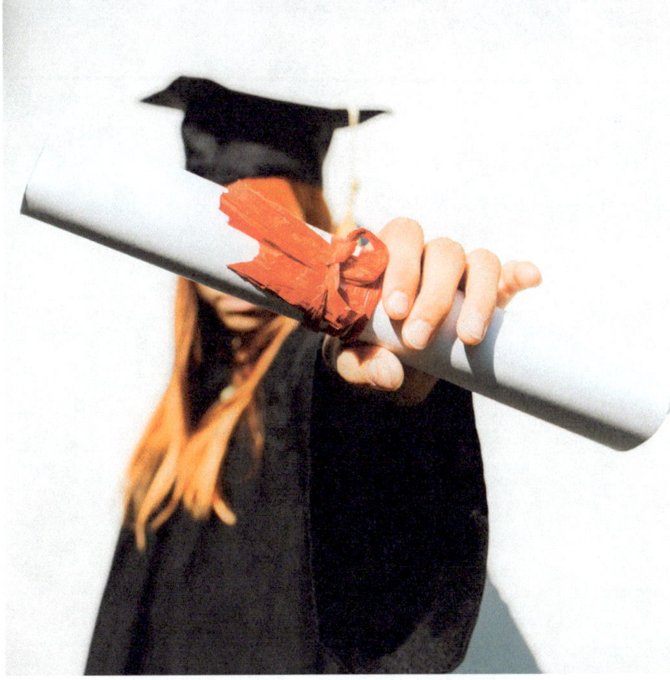
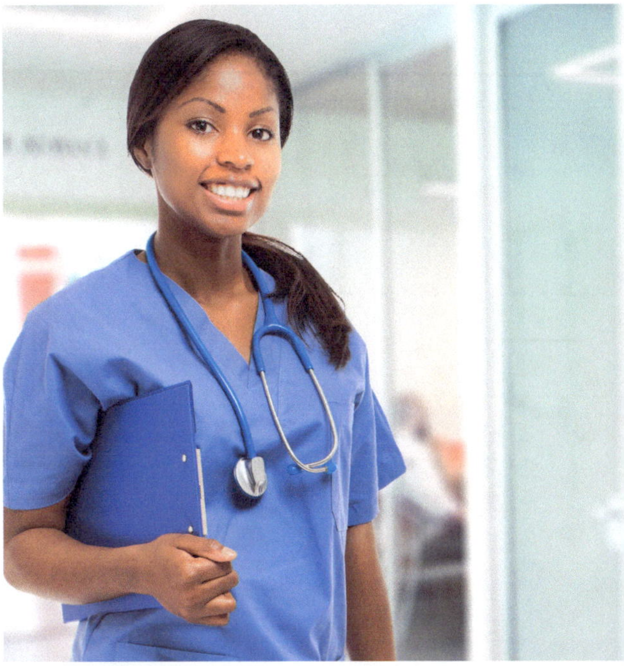

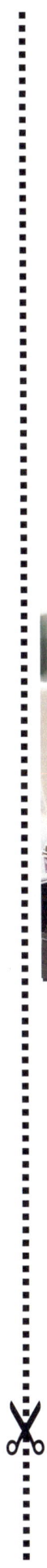

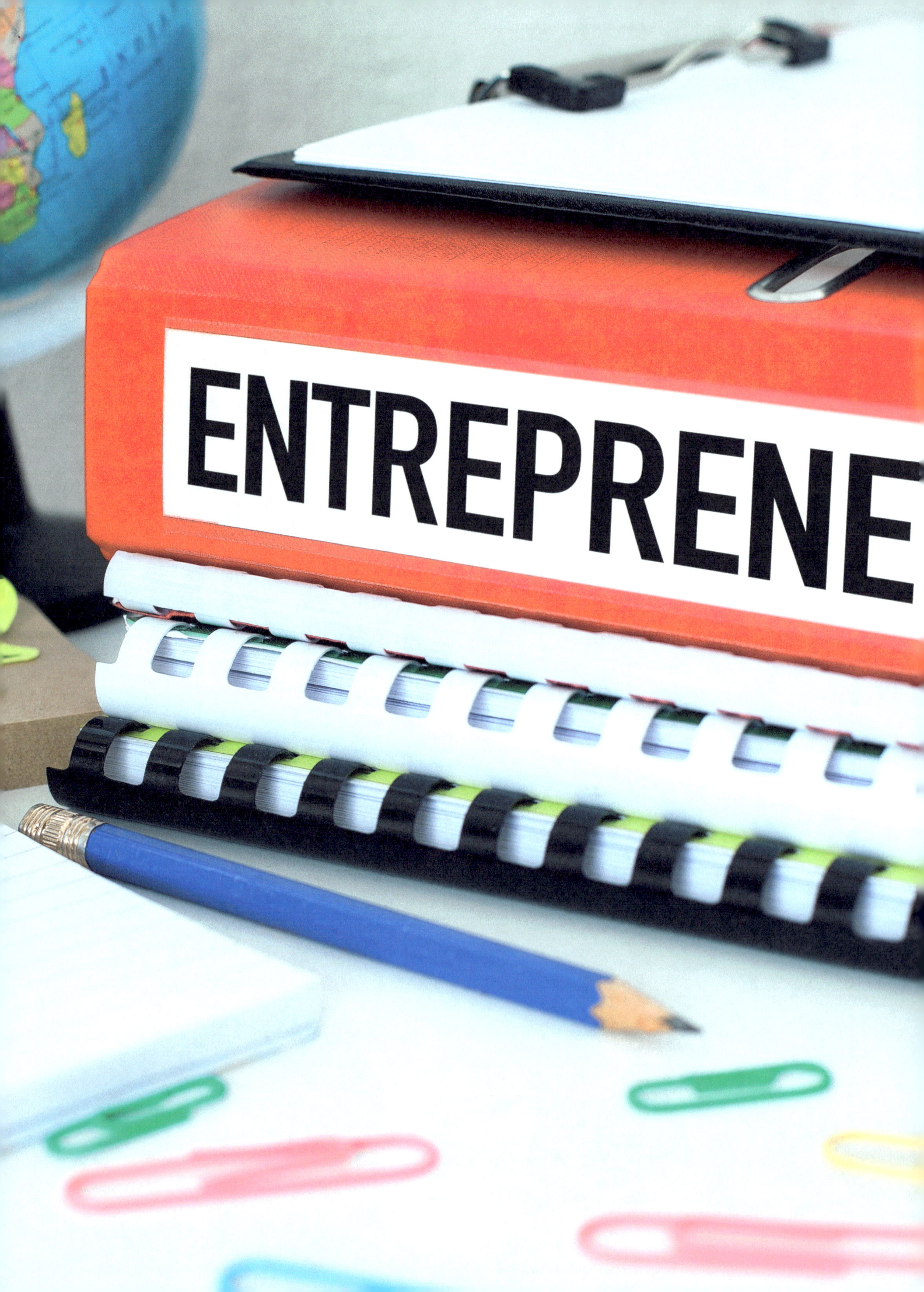
ENTREPRENE

CONTENT CREATOR

PRIKOL BANK 10000
DOLLARS
THIS NOTE IS LEGAL TENDER
ALL DEBTS, PUBLIC AND PRIVATE
SERIES 2006 A
Treasurer of the United States.
Secretary of the Treasury.
KB 90490962
HUNDRED DOLLARS
100

Pay off Debts

DEBT FREE
PROCESS...

SAVE   INVEST

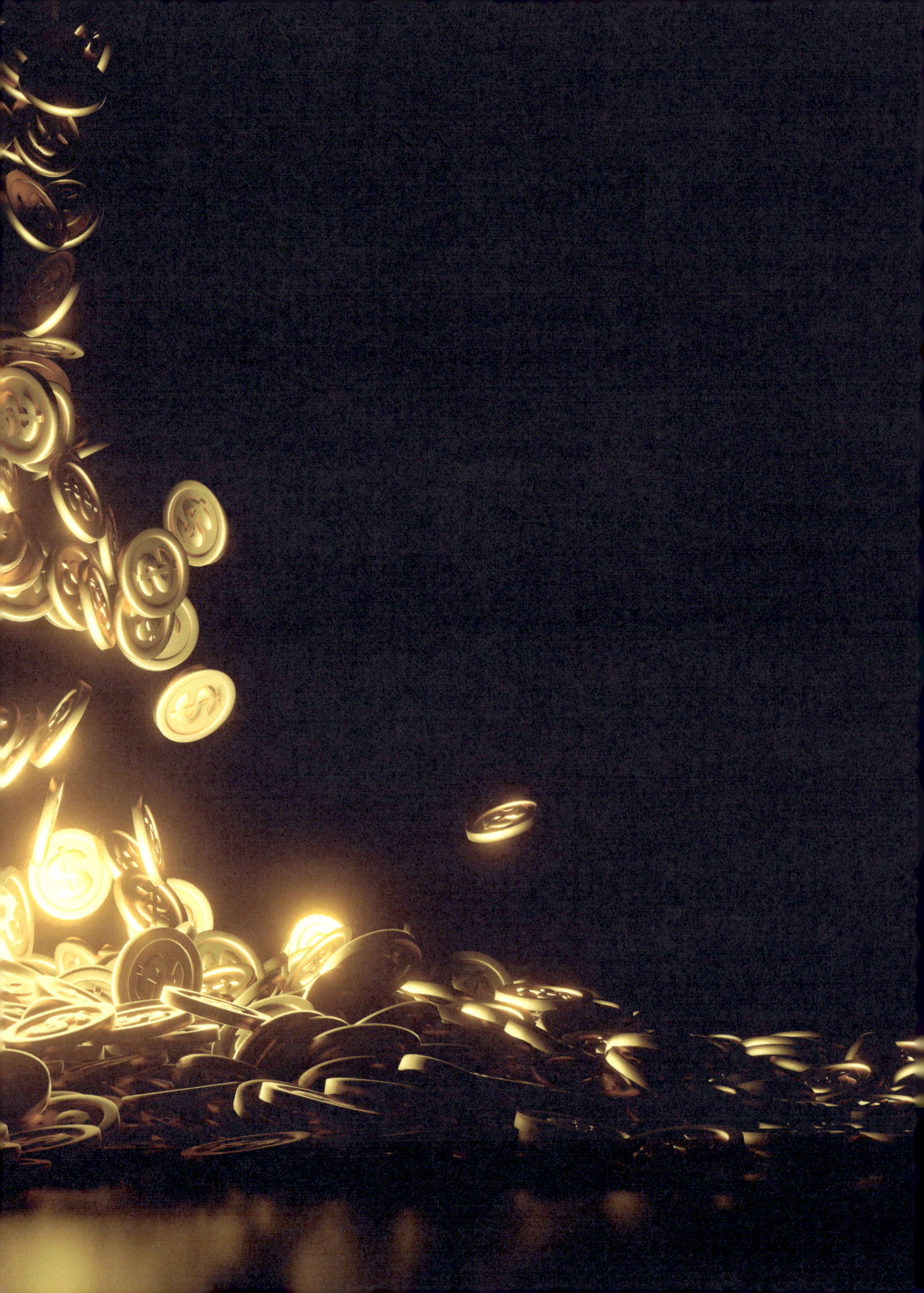

| Your name _____ | Bank of Abundance | 0123 |

Date _____ 20 ___

Pay to the order of _____ $ _____

_____ dollars

Security features included details on back

Memo
_____

:012345678 :0123 :01234

**Not for literal use but for motivational purposes

If you could travel anywhere in the world, where would you go? Fill out your boarding pass below.

BOARDING PASS | **BOARDING PASS**

VIP PASS | **VIP PASS**

FOCUS

Wealth Wonders

"Money, I've learned, is freedom in material form." - Aja Brown, former Mayor of Compton, California

Reflect on how you define wealth in your own life. How does this definition influence your goals and actions, and in what ways can you cultivate a sense of abundance beyond just financial wealth?"

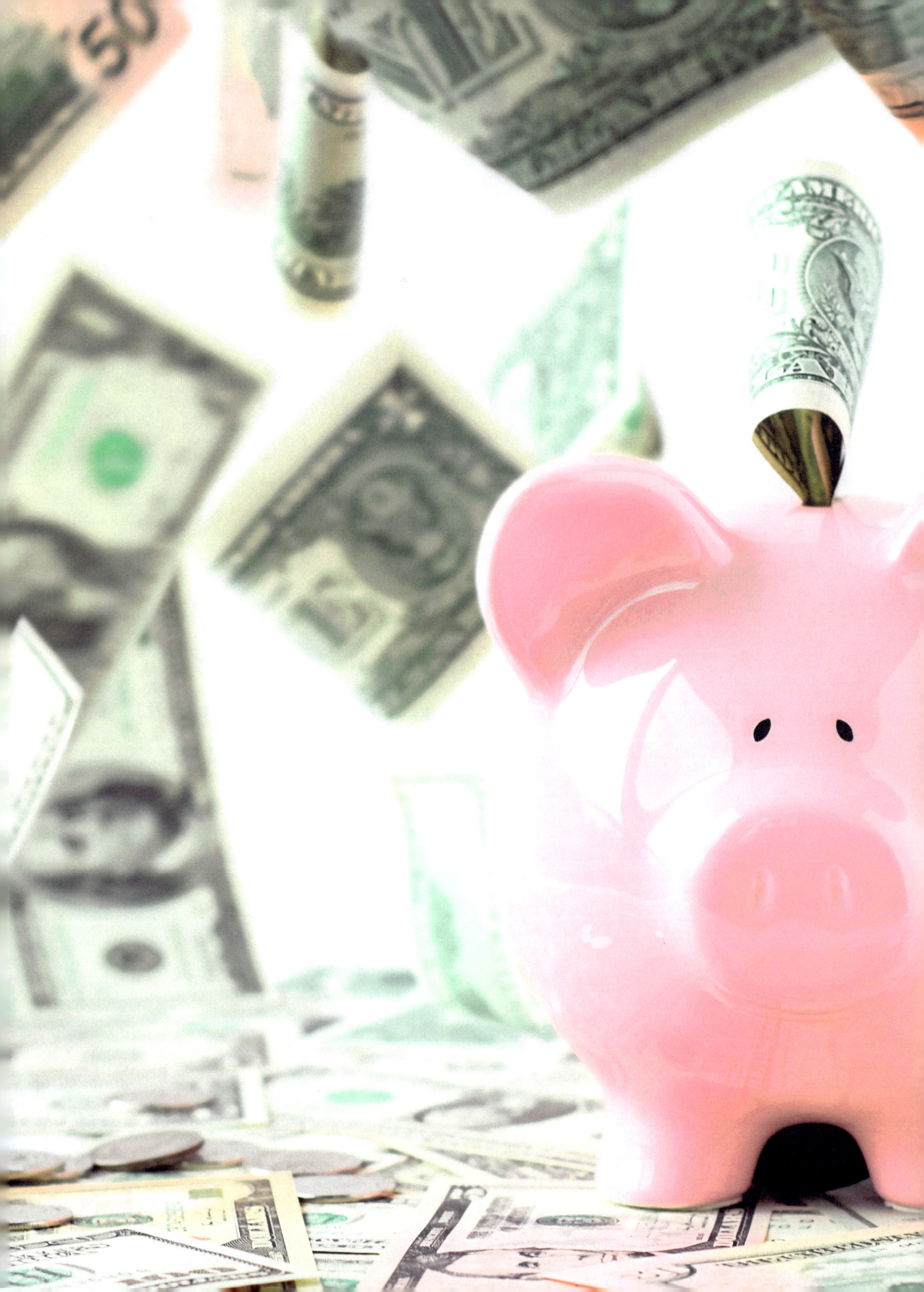

- Make Yourself Proud
- Great things up ahead 
- I DESERVE A GOOD NIGHT'S SLEEP 
- True Happiness is inside of me 
- MAKE today GREAT 
- LOVE Yourself
- NEVER Stop growing
- Be Positive 
- Embrace my potential & Exceed my expectations 
- DOING my BEST 
- It's going to be a good day 
- I Trust My Inner Choice 
- My Brain is Strong 
- trust your JOURNEY 
- Be Free

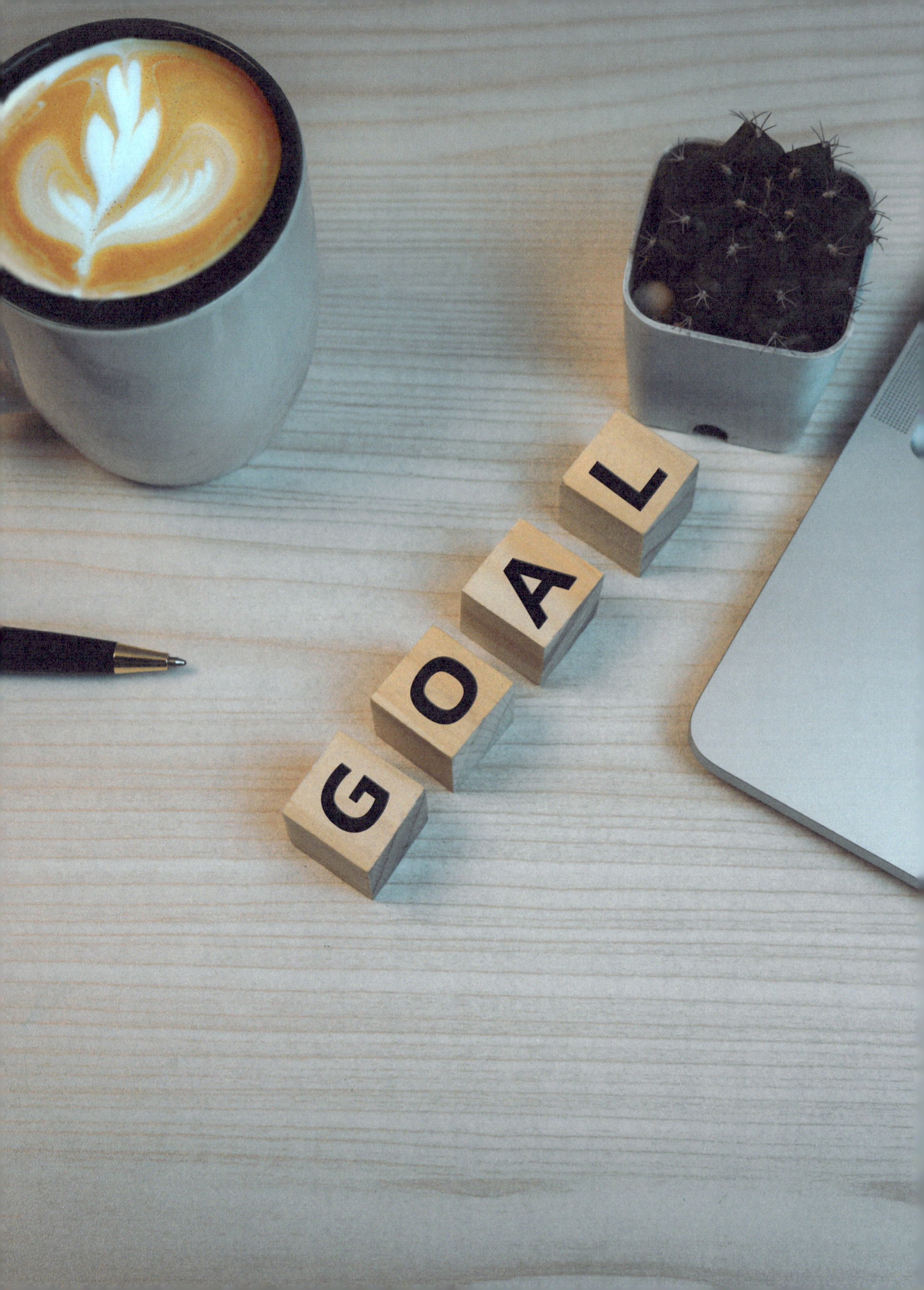
GOAL

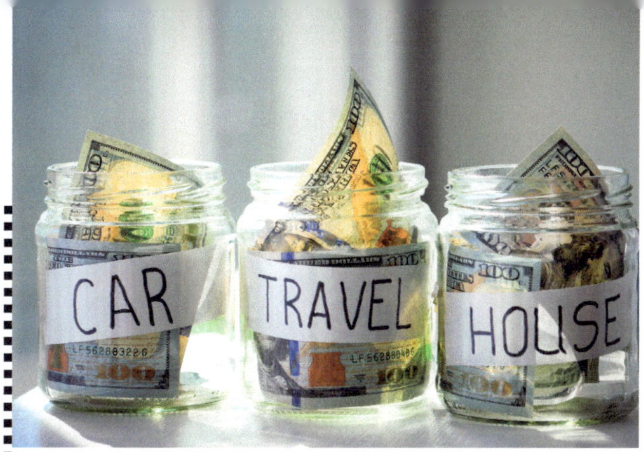
CAR
TRAVEL
HOUSE

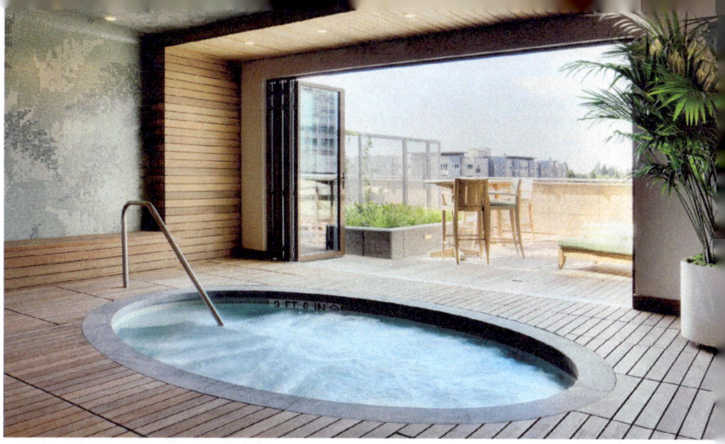

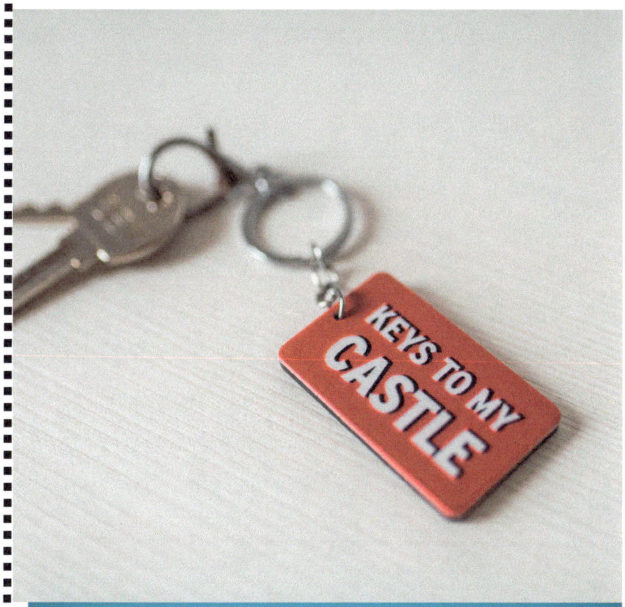
KEYS TO MY CASTLE

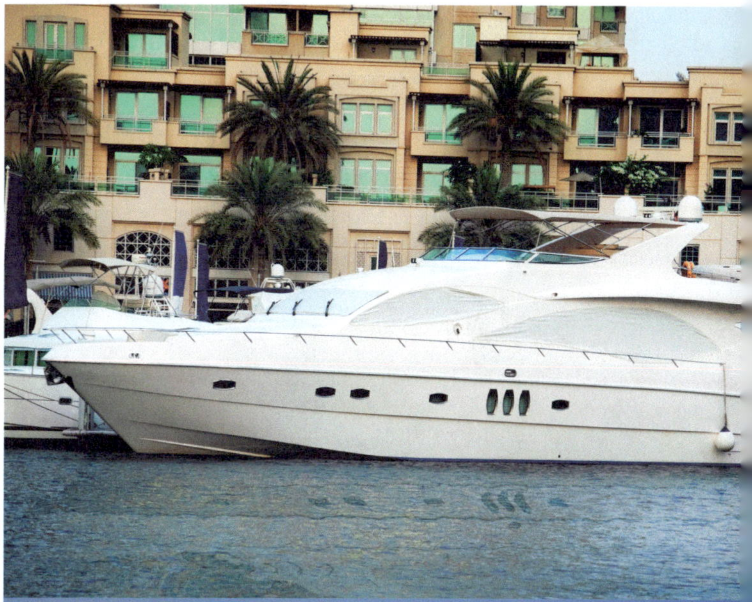

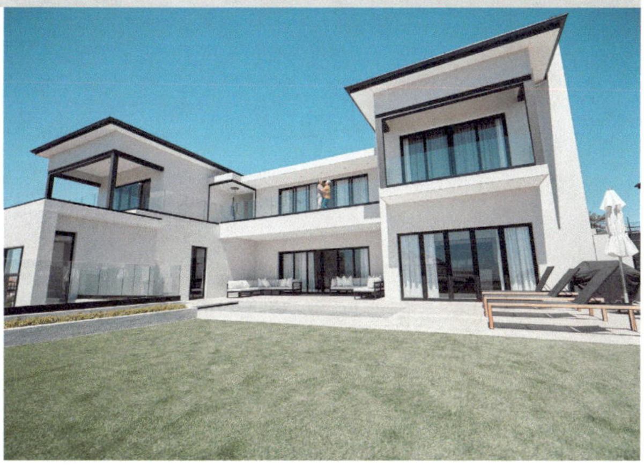

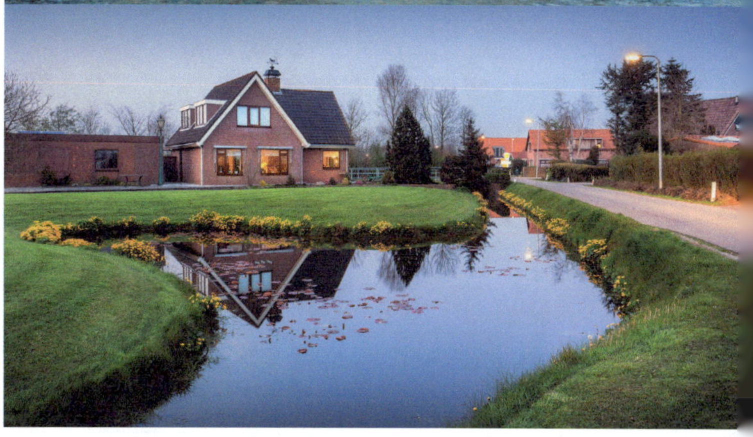

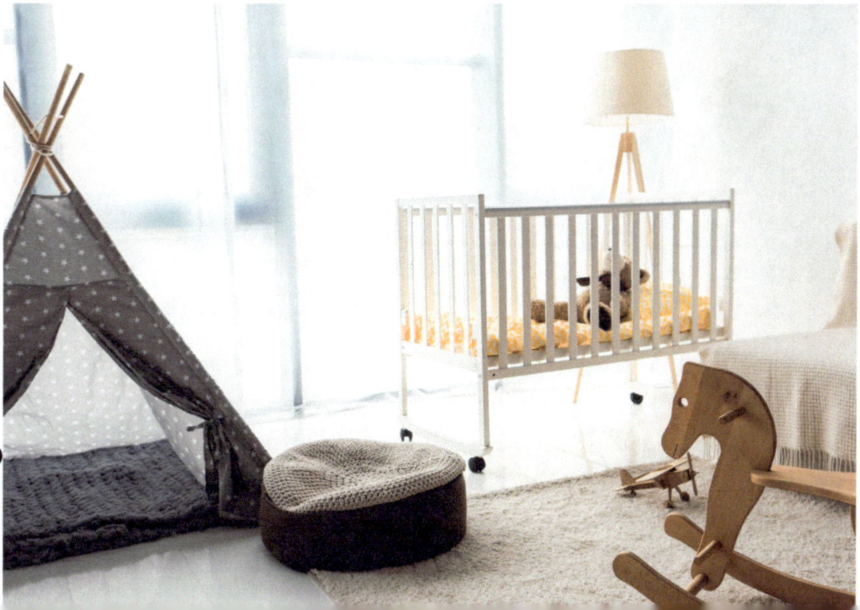

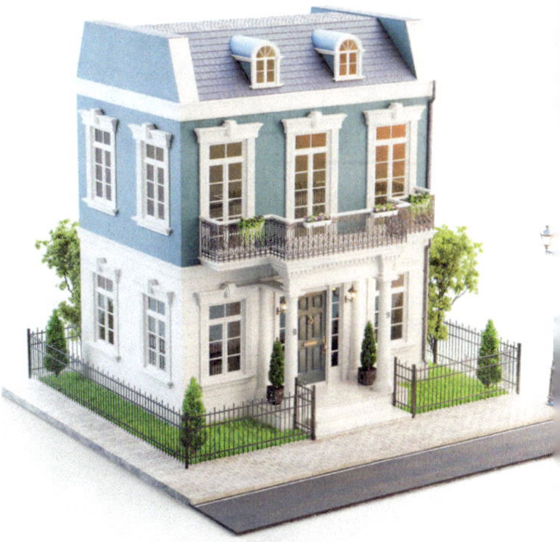

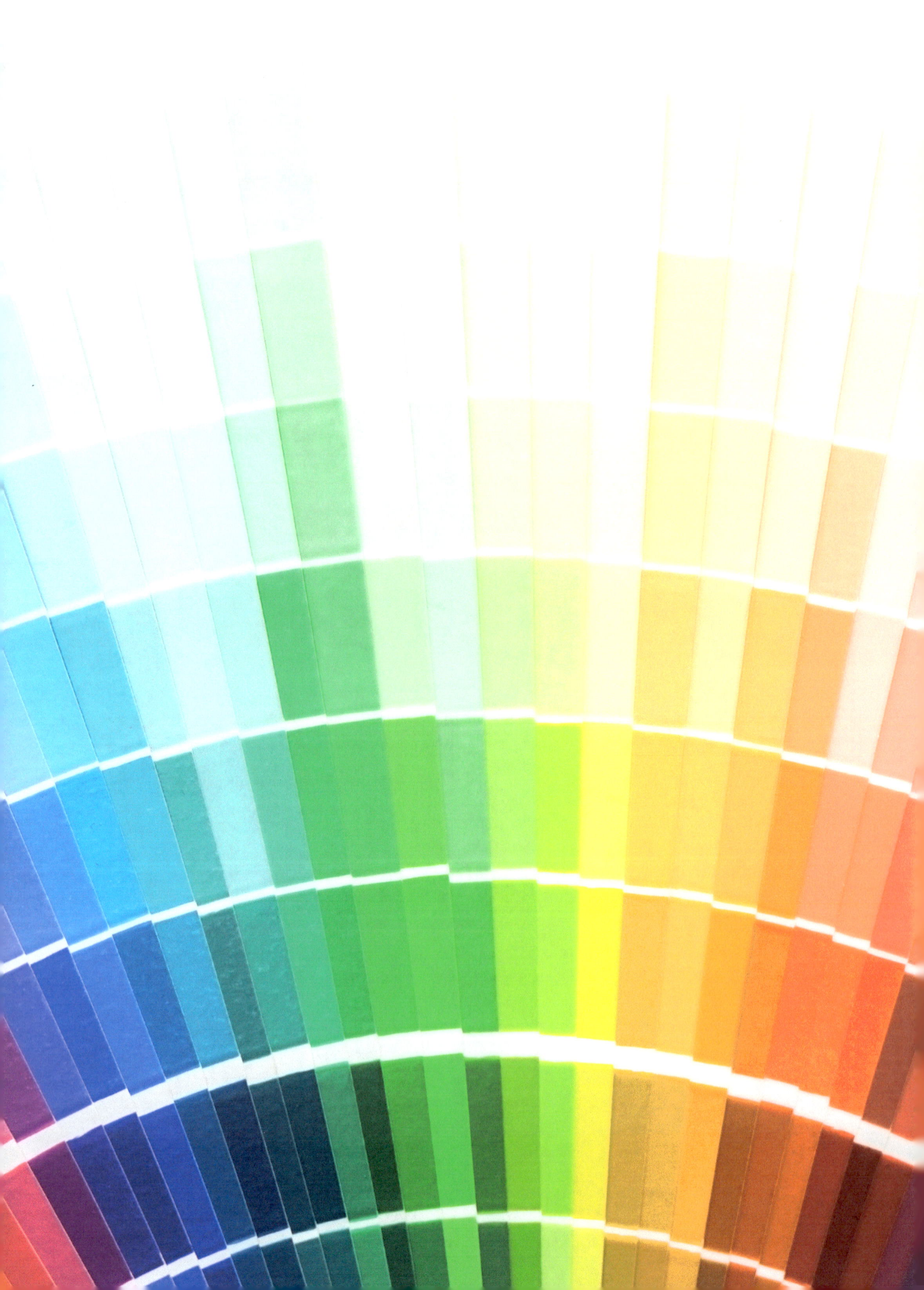

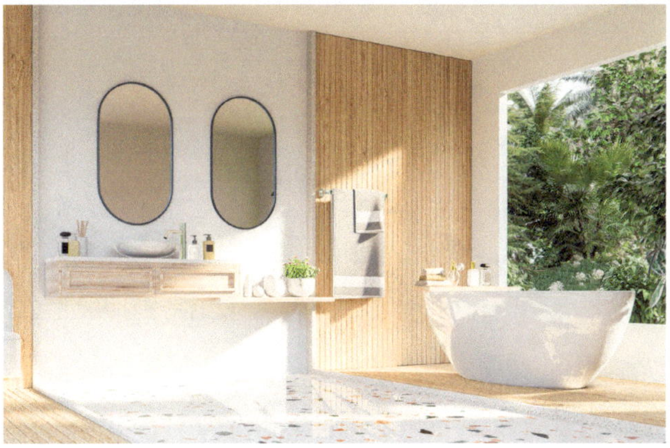
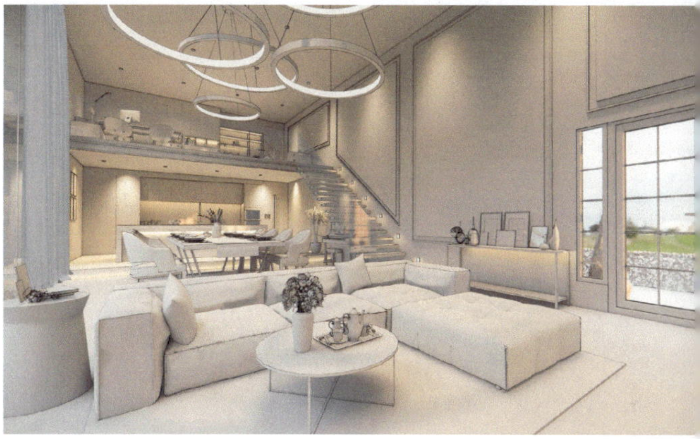
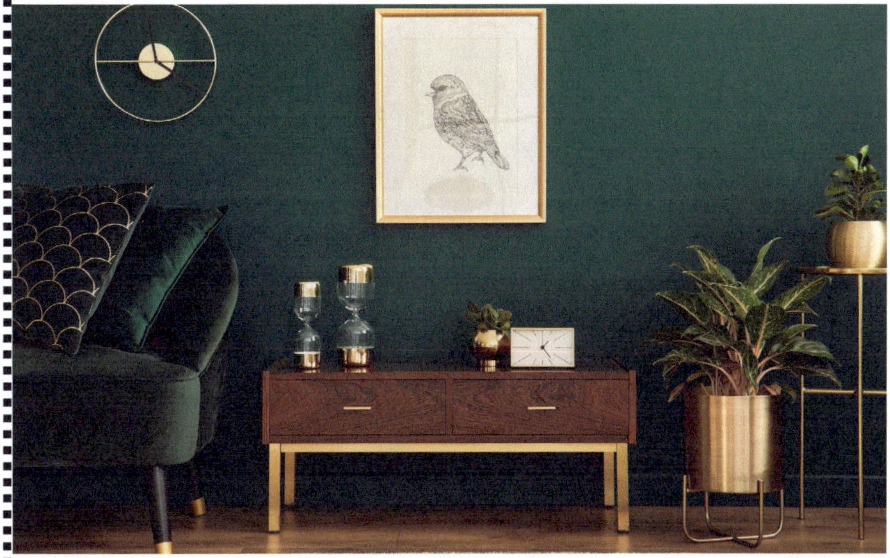
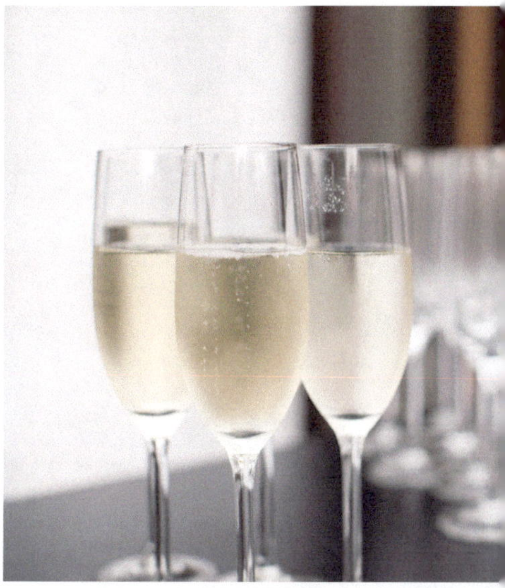
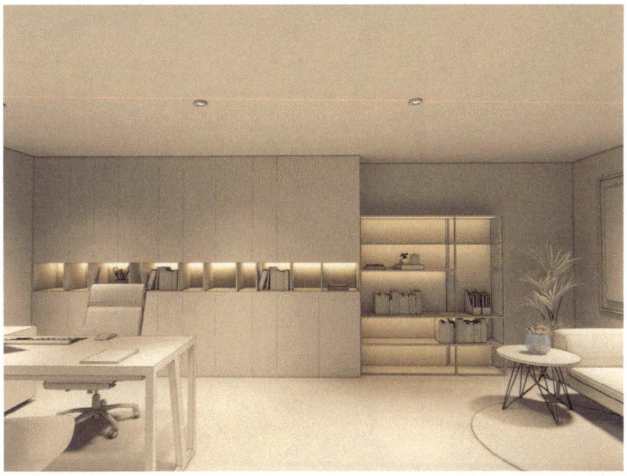
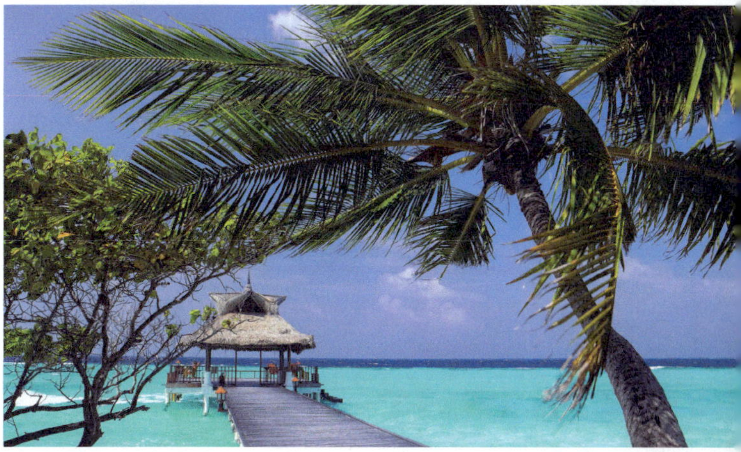
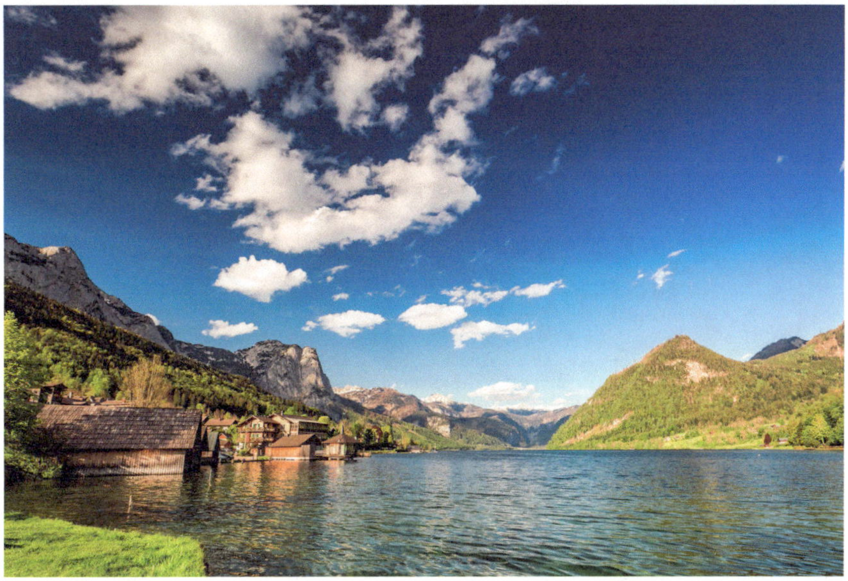
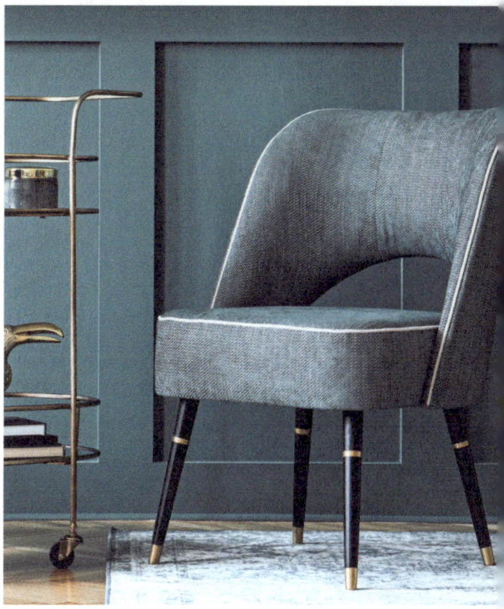

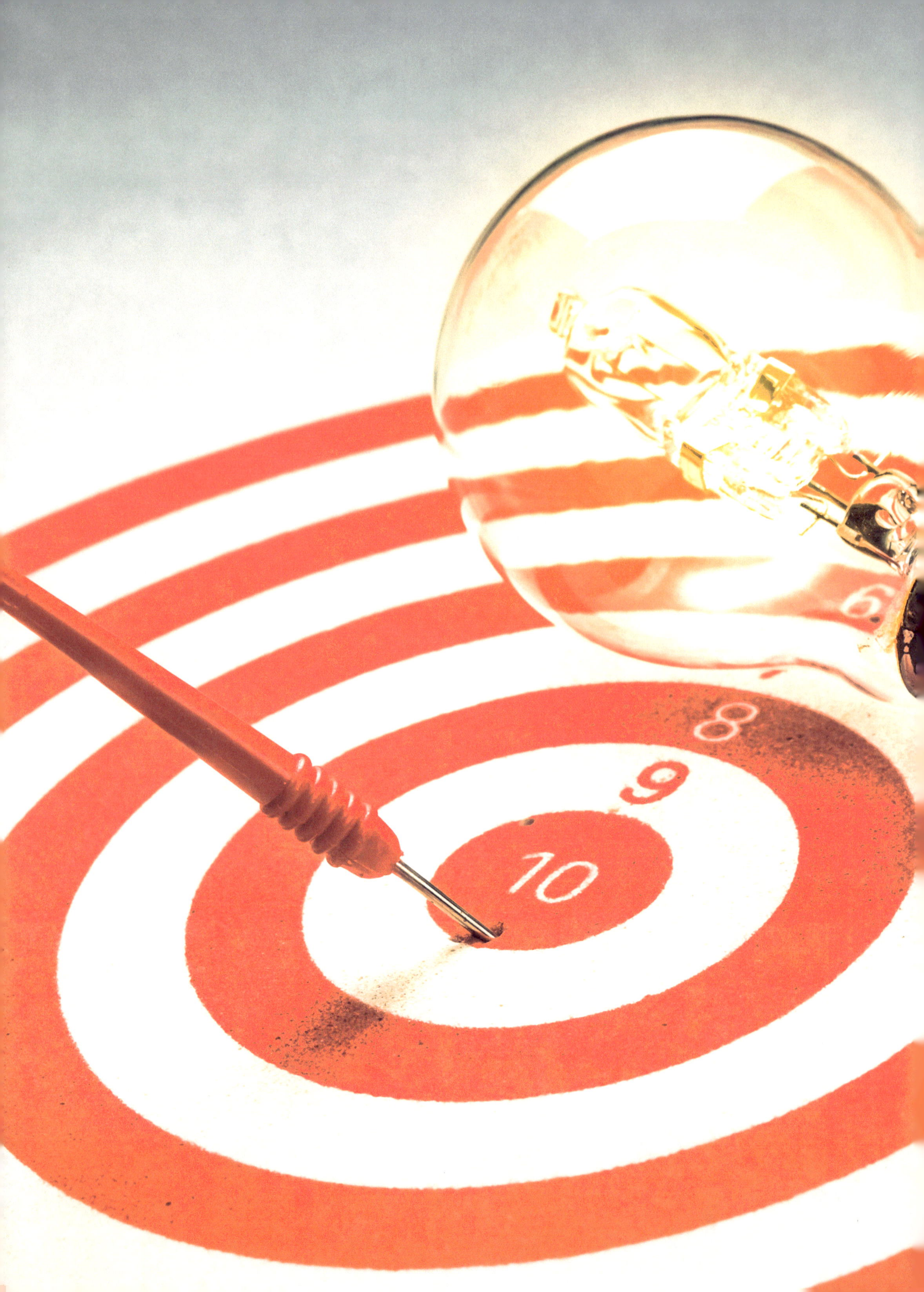
8
9
10

- My life is just beginning
- I am worthy of all the good things that happen in my life. 
- My thoughts are filled with positivity and my life is plentiful with prosperity.
- My obstacles are moving out of my way; my path is carved towards greatness.   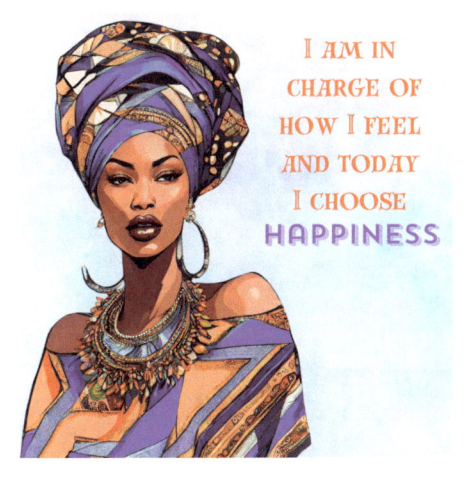
- My potential to succeed is limitless
- I am the architect of my life: I build its foundation and choose its contents.
- I AM IN CHARGE OF HOW I FEEL AND TODAY I CHOOSE HAPPINESS
- "Love is not just a feeling; it's an action that shows how much you care, every single day"   
- I wake up today with strength in my heart and clarity in my mind.
- I CHOOSE to be proud of myself and the things I CHOOSE to do
- I AM A BEACON OF LOVE AND COMPASSION
- The only way to achieve the impossible is to believe it is possible

GET RID OF EVERYTHING THAT DOES NOT MATTER

LESS IS MORE

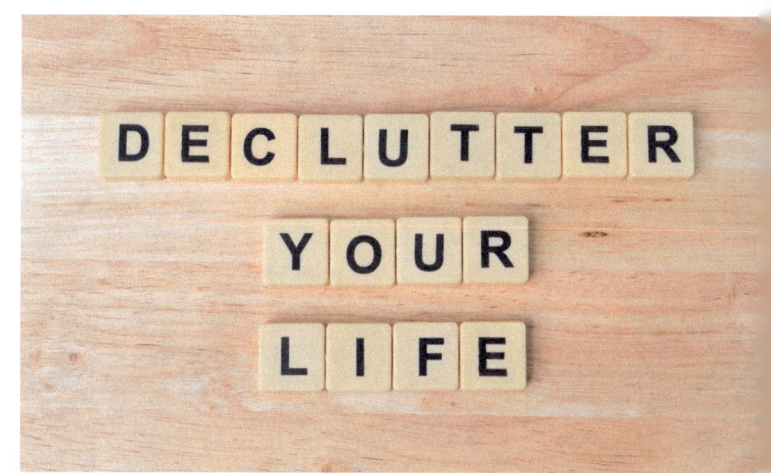

DECLUTTER YOUR LIFE

ATLANTIC
AZORES (Port.)
Horta
MADEIRA IS. (Port.)
CANARY IS. (Sp.)
CAPE VERDE ISLANDS (Port.)
Praia
PORTUGAL
Lisboa
Porto
Lagos
SPAIN
Madrid
Granada
Gibraltar
FRANCE
Paris
Bilbao
Marseille
Barcelona
Bay of Biscay
MEDITERRANEAN
Sardinia
Alger
Oran
Constantine
Tunis
TUNISIA
Sfax
MOROCCO
Fez
Rabat
Figuig
Touggourt
Bou Garfa
ALGERIA
In Salah
In Ziza
Alghan
Tit
Tripoli
Gadames
Sebha
Murzuch
LIBIA
EGYPT
Tummo
Djado
Bardai
Tombouctou
Niafounke
Bamako
Ségou
Niger
Gao
Agades
Niamey
Zinder
L. Chad
Bissau
GUINEA
Freetown
SIERRA LEONE (Br.)
Monrovia
LIBERIA
Korhogo
GOLD COAST (Br.)
Abidjan
Accra
Lomé
Lagos
Idah
Kano
NIGERIA (Br.)
CAMEROONS
Yaoundé
Santa Isabel
SP. GUINEA
EQUATORIAL AFRICA
Ft. Lamy
ANGLO-EGYPTIAN SUDAN
Mayombe
(Port.) CABINDA
Santo Antônio
Luanda
Novo Redondo
Benguela
ANGOLA
BELG. CONGO
FR.
30

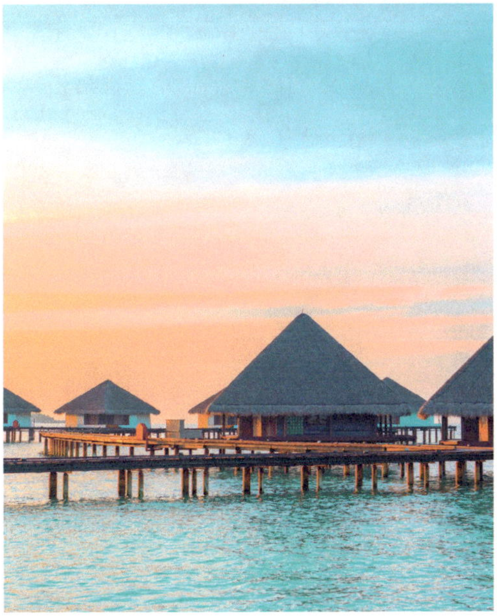
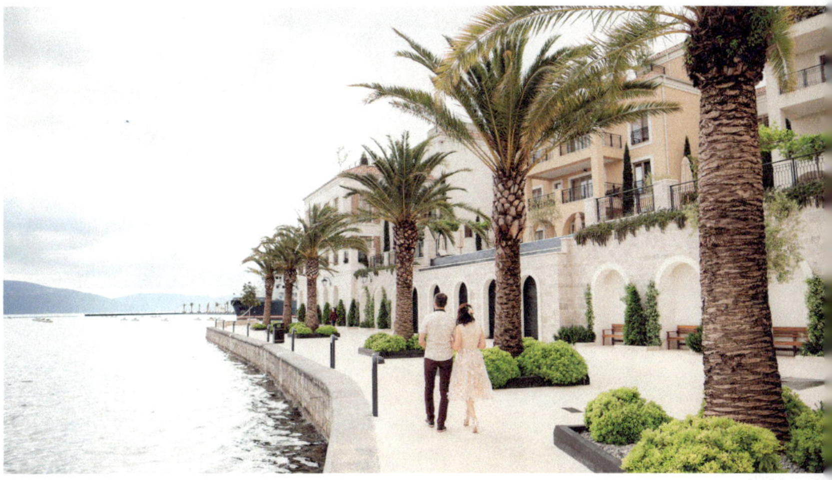
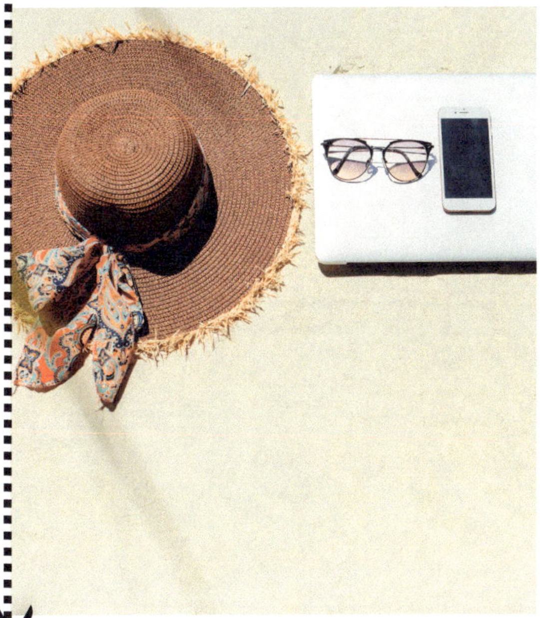
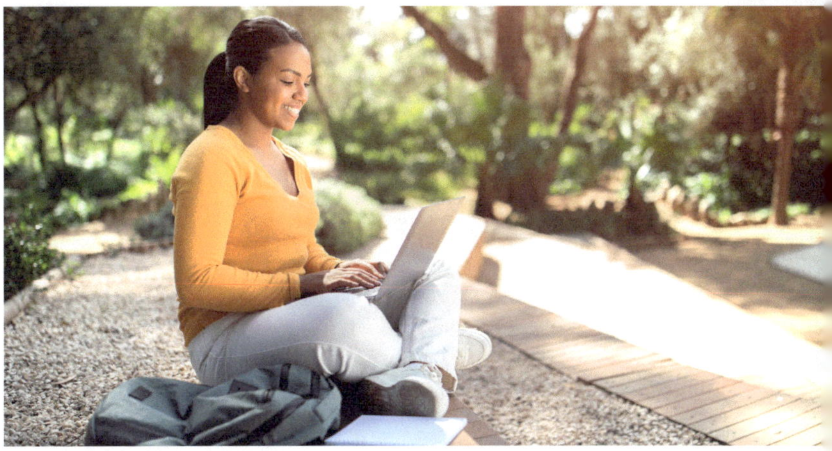
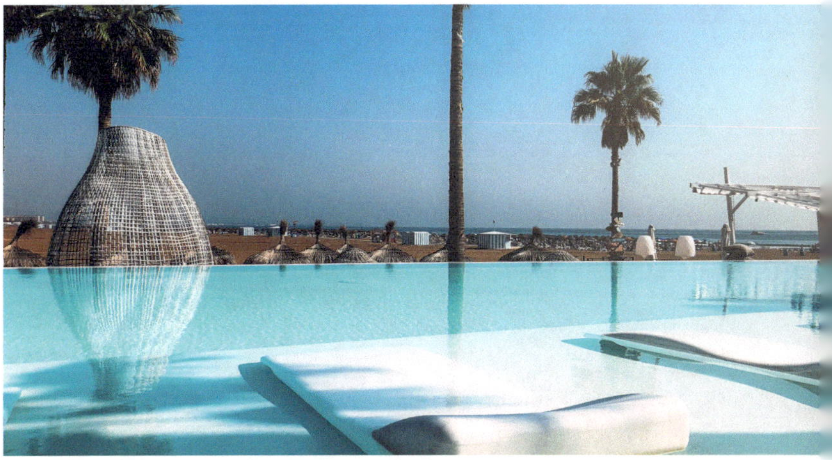
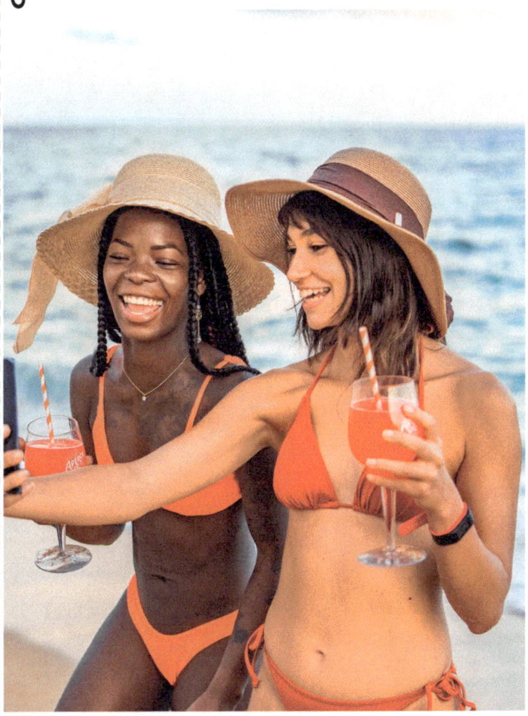
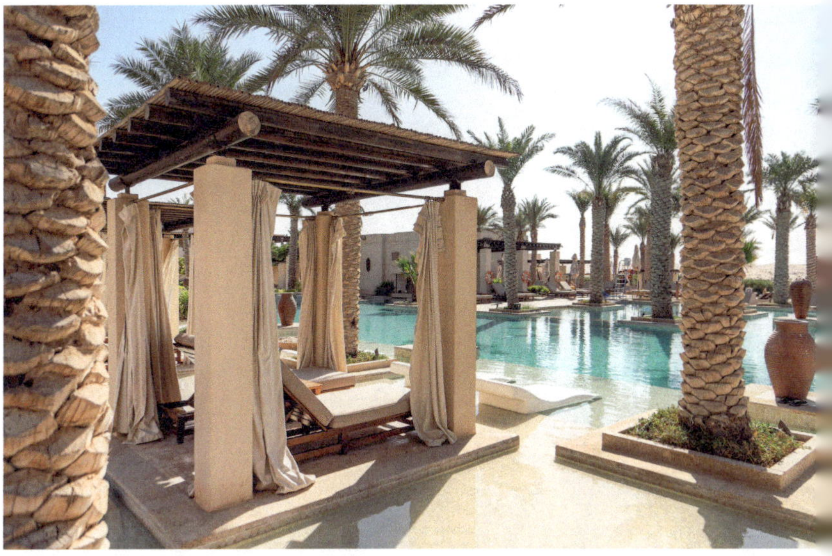

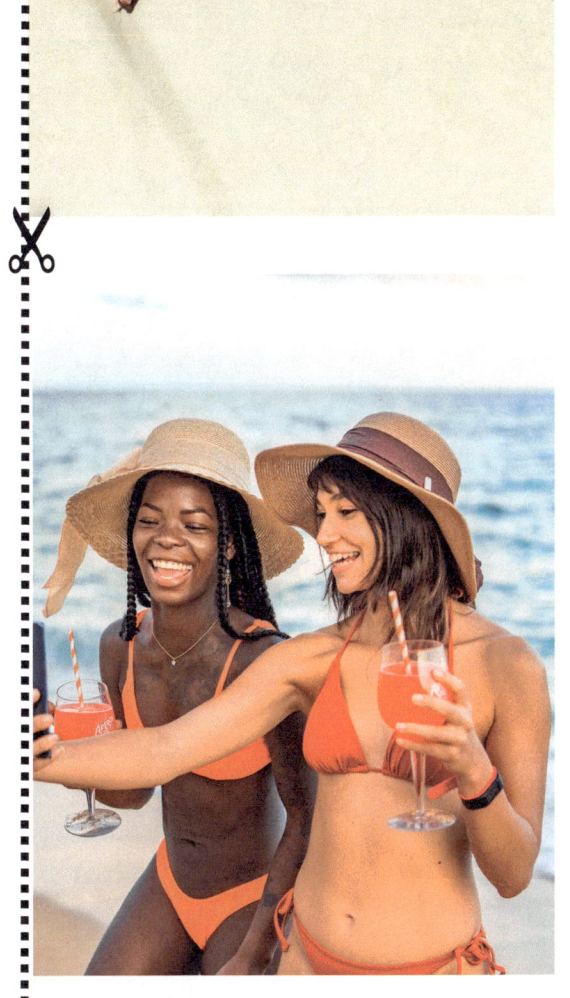

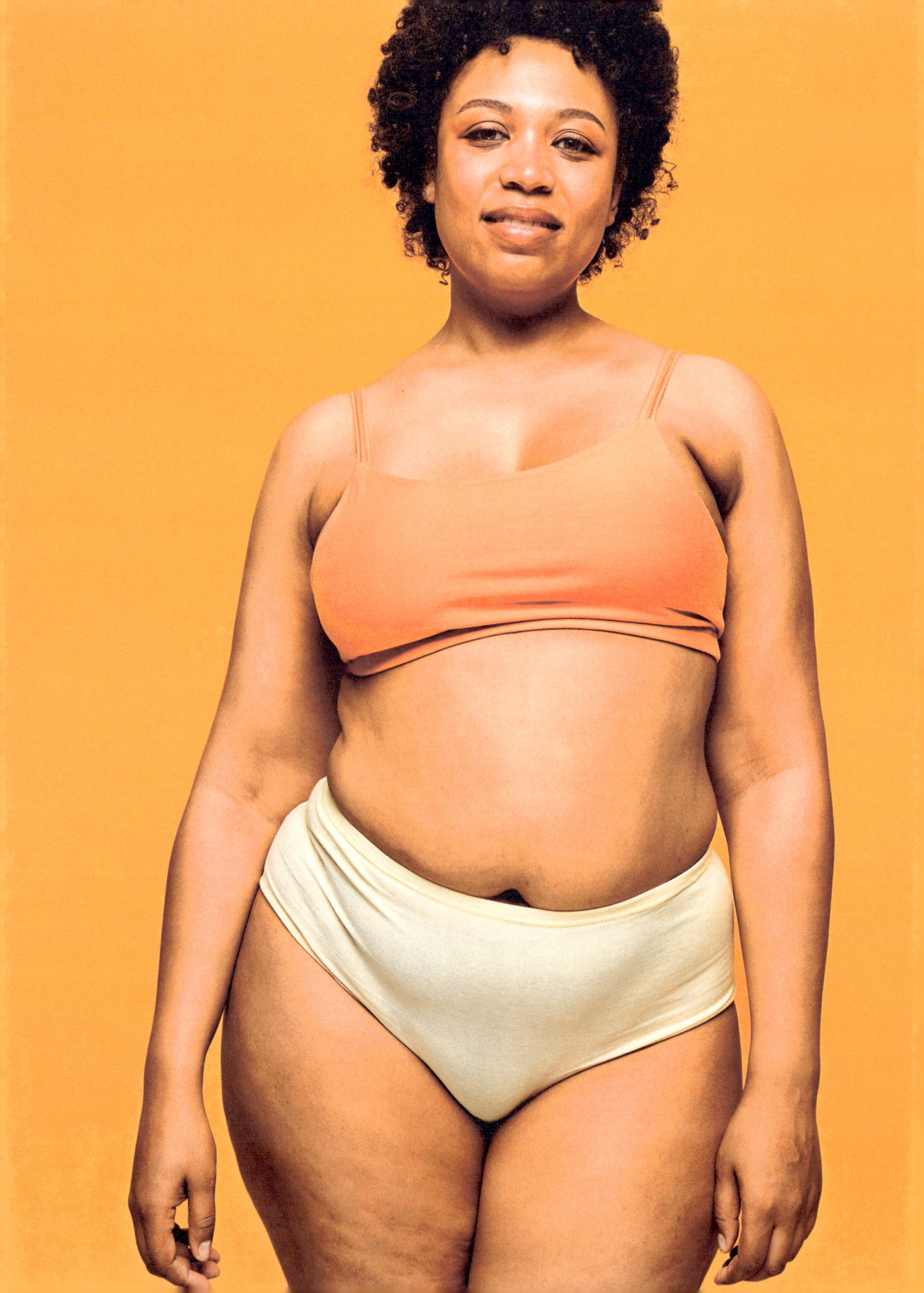

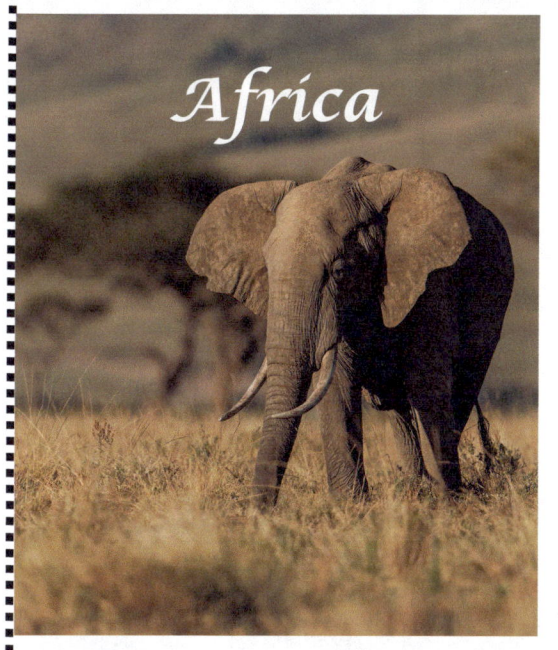

Africa

Aurora Borealis

Venice

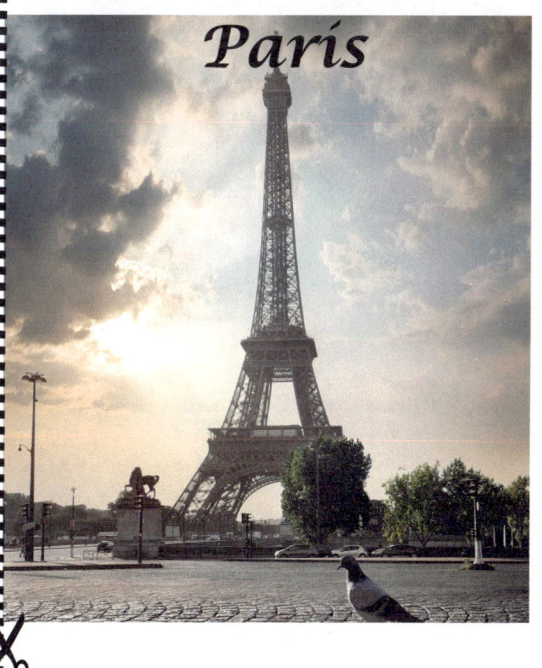

Paris

Machu Picchu, Peru

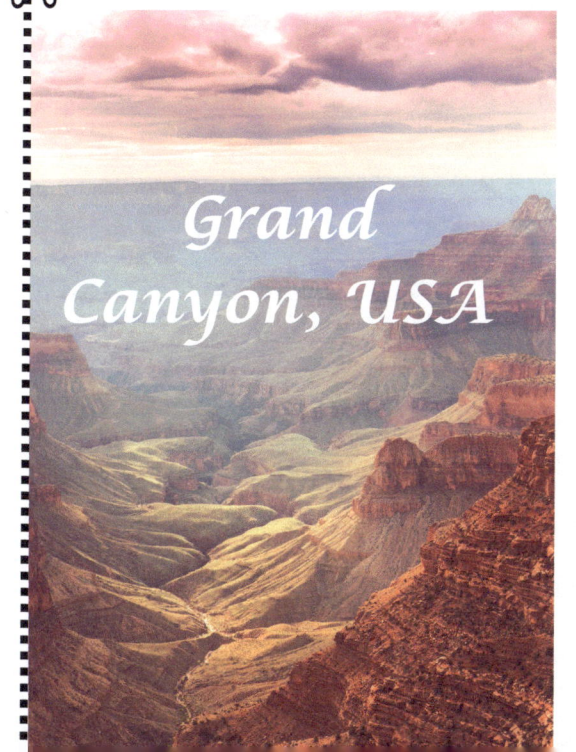

Grand Canyon, USA

Australia

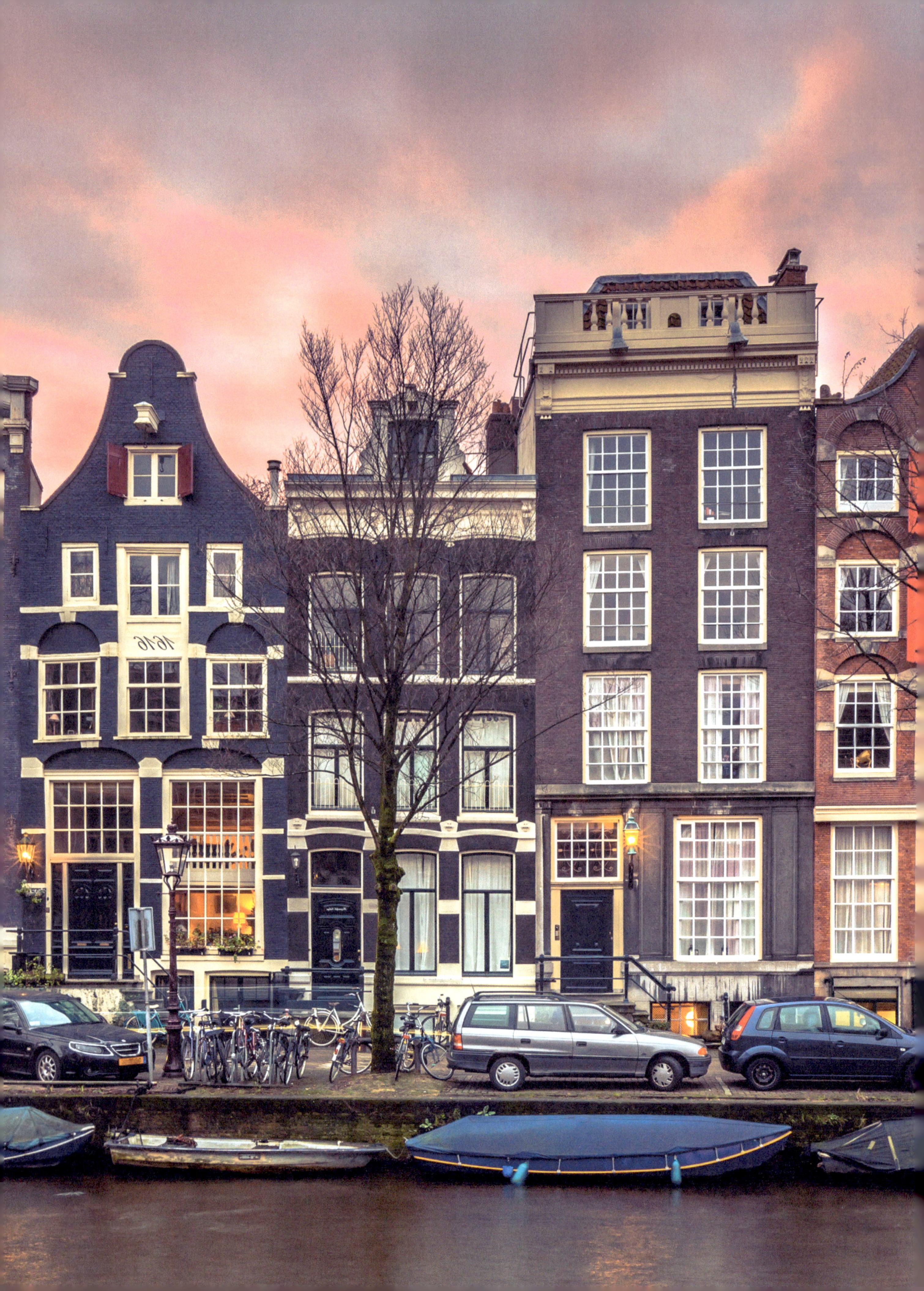

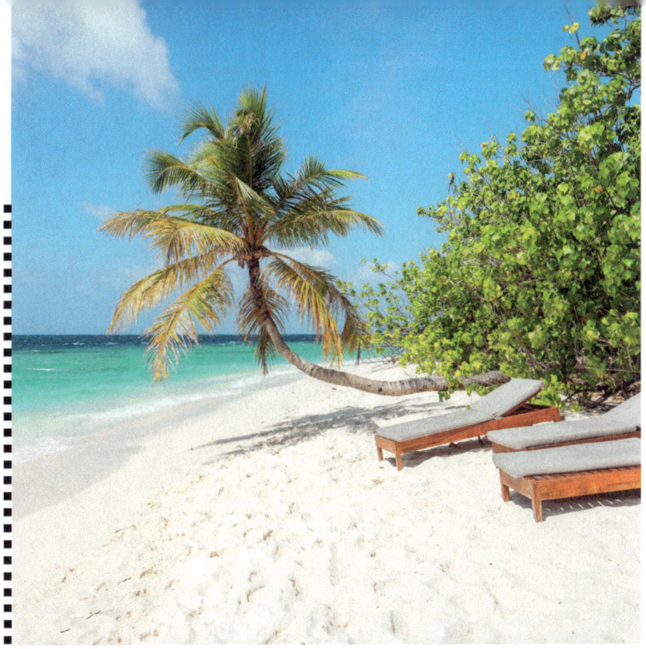
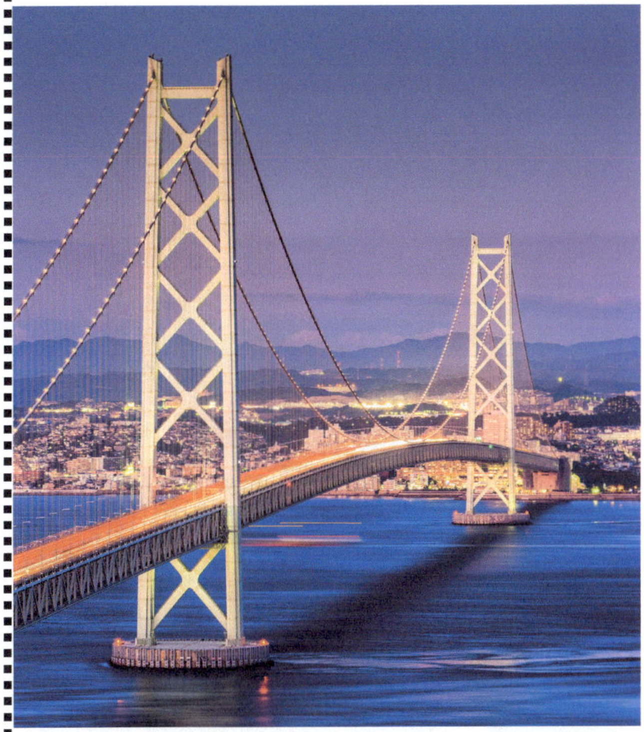
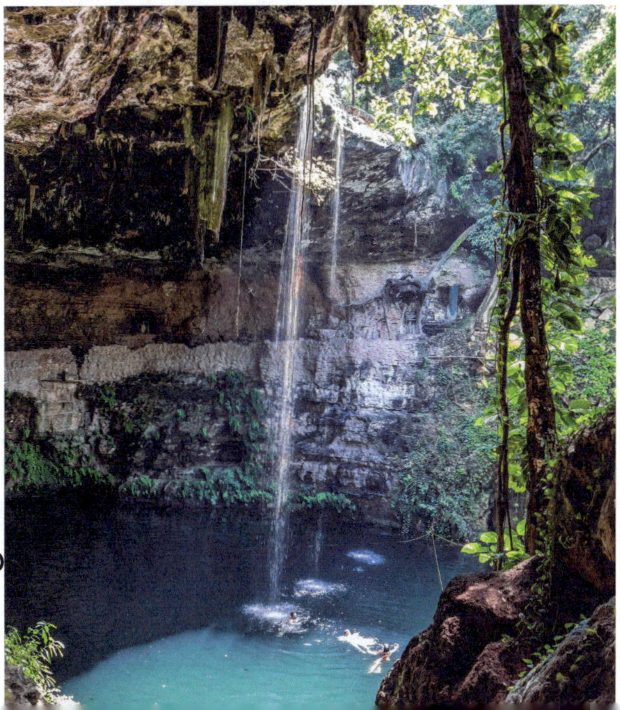
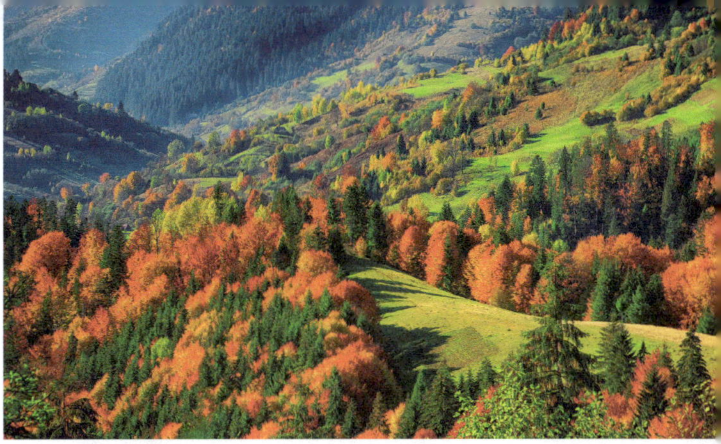
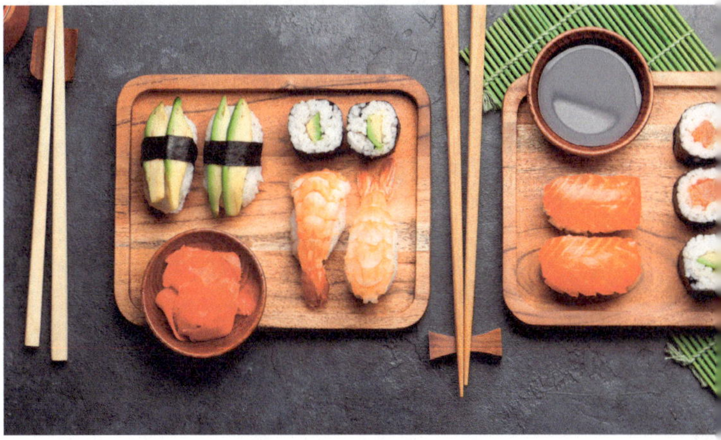
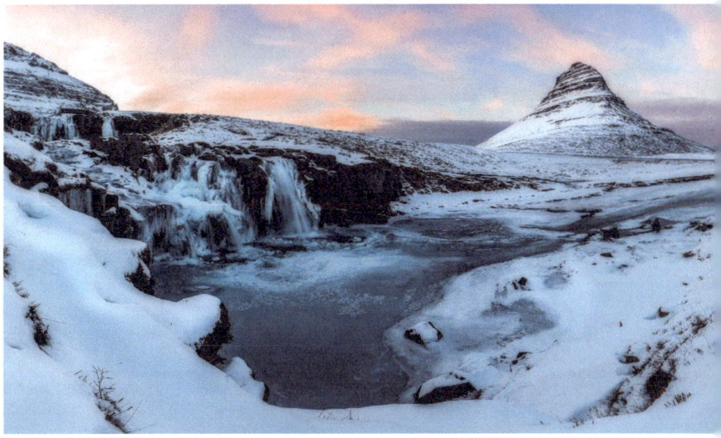
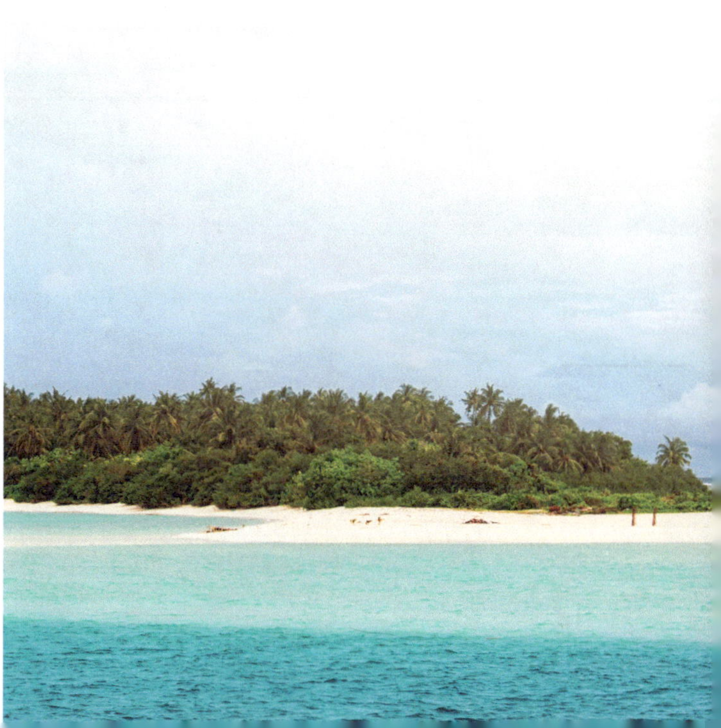

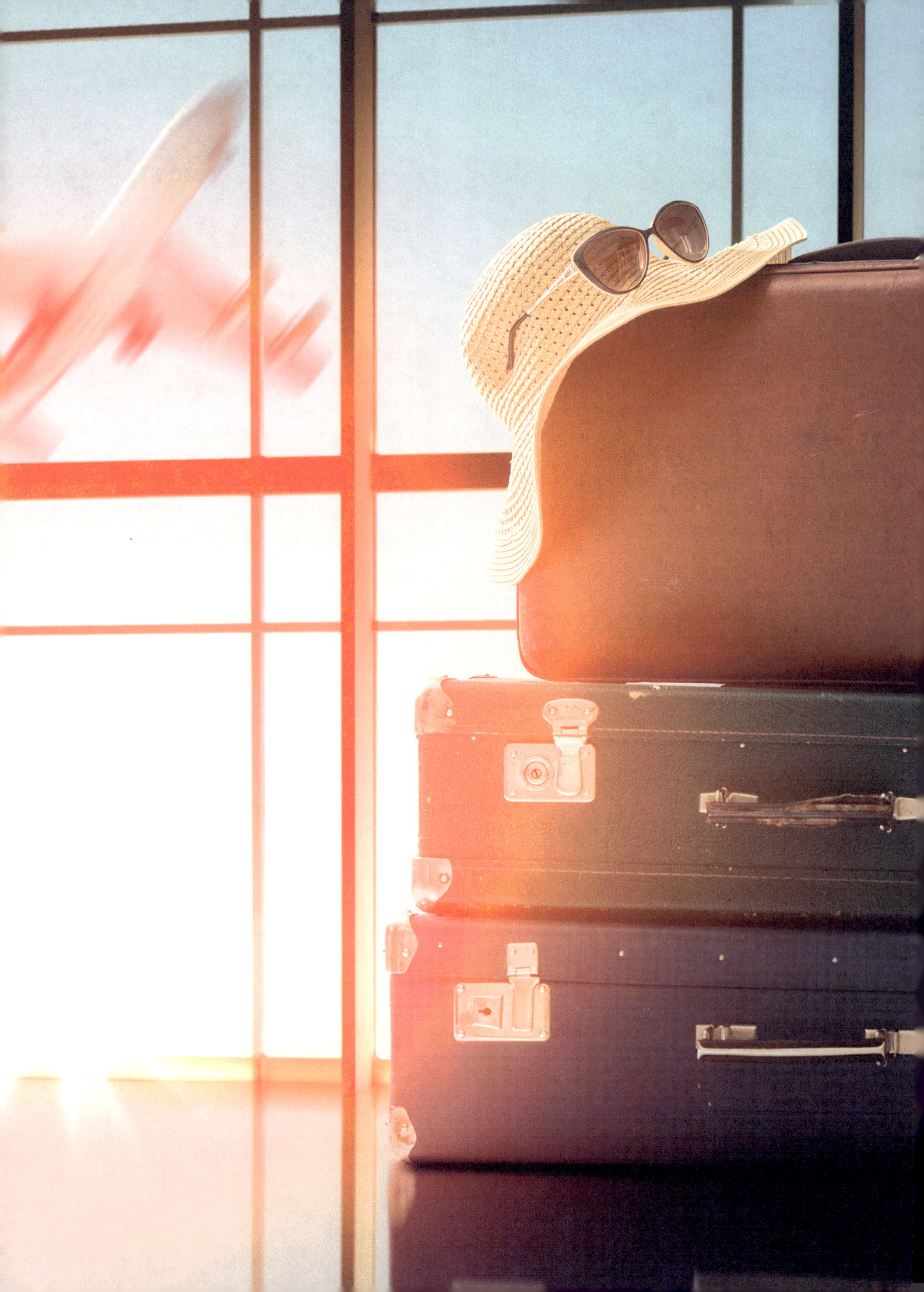

- Wow!!!
- No One Is Perfect
- love
- YES I CAN
- hello
- noted
- yay!
- Anything is possible
- NEVER GIVE UP
- ONE DAY at a time
- but first COFFEE
- ON THE Road
- PRIORITY
- yes!
- No!
- OK!
- REMINDER
- HAPPY
- I AM ME!
- This is my life
- Trust Yourself
- What a wonderful day
- ALWAYS SMILING
- FOLLOW YOUR DREAMS

GRL PWR

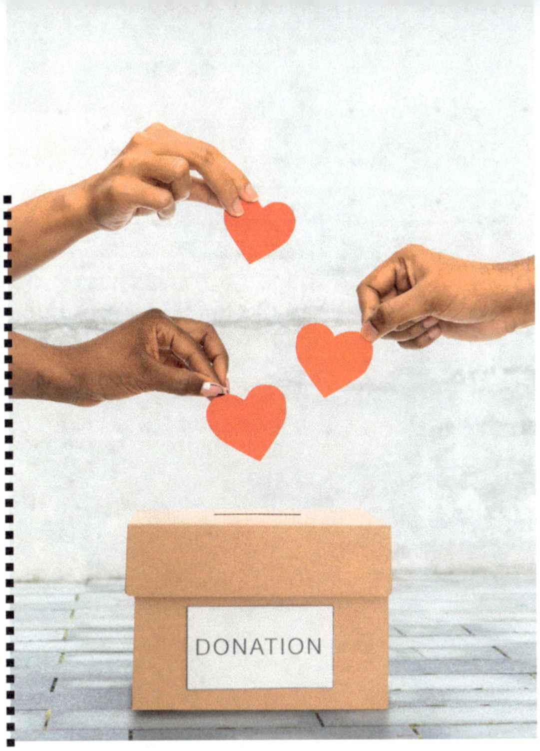
DONATION

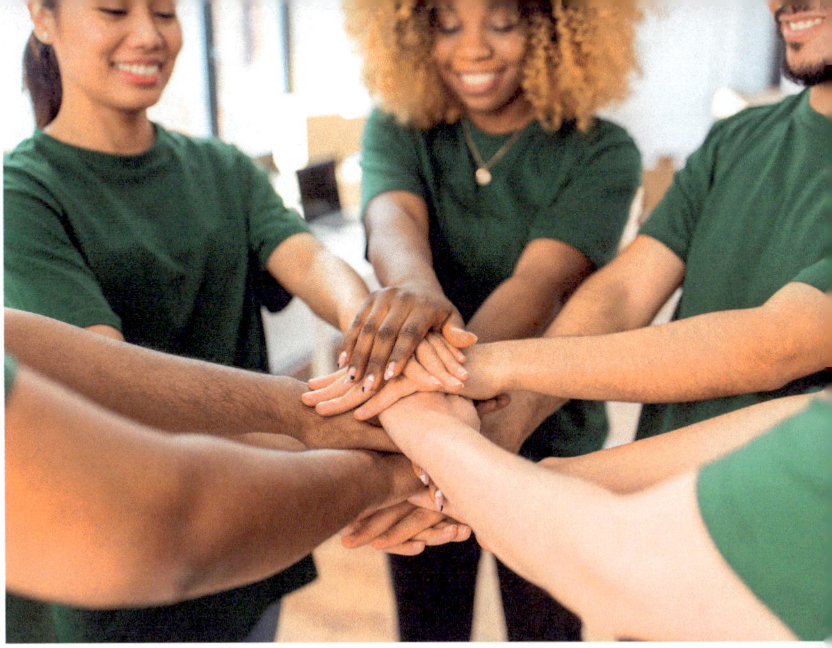

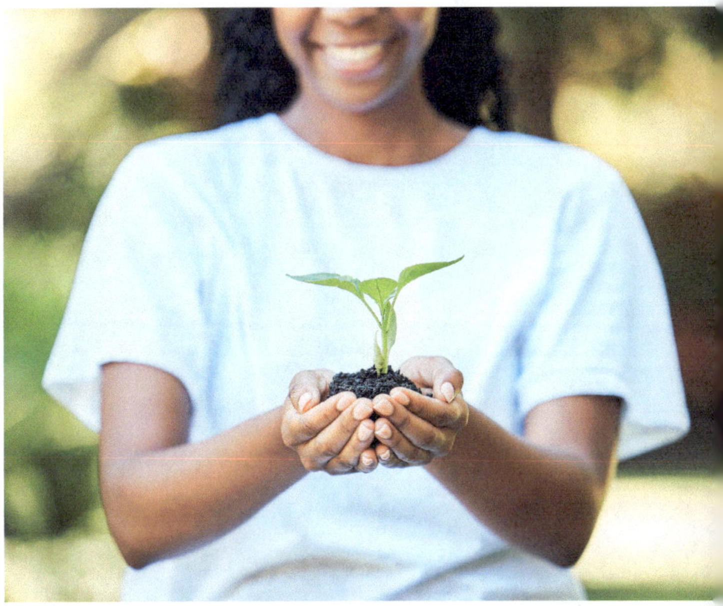

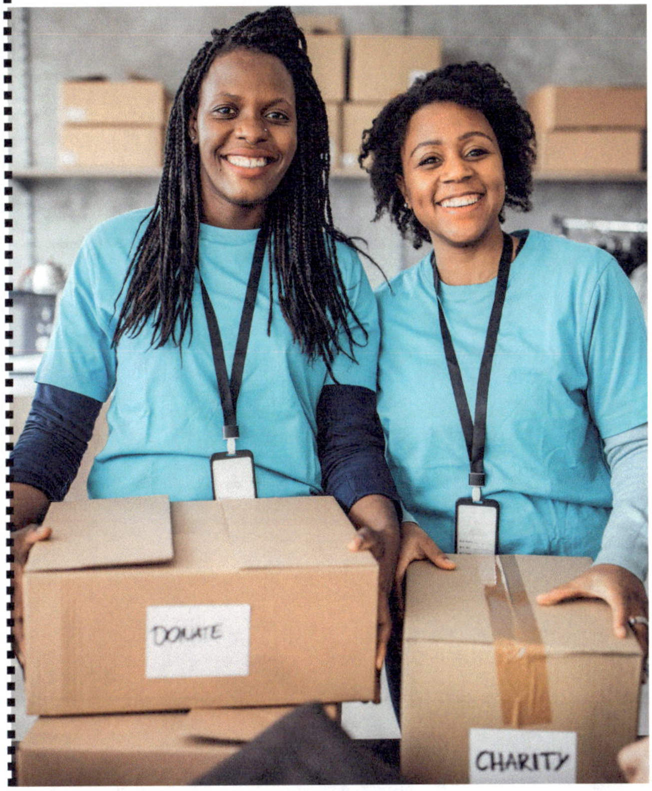
DONATE
CHARITY

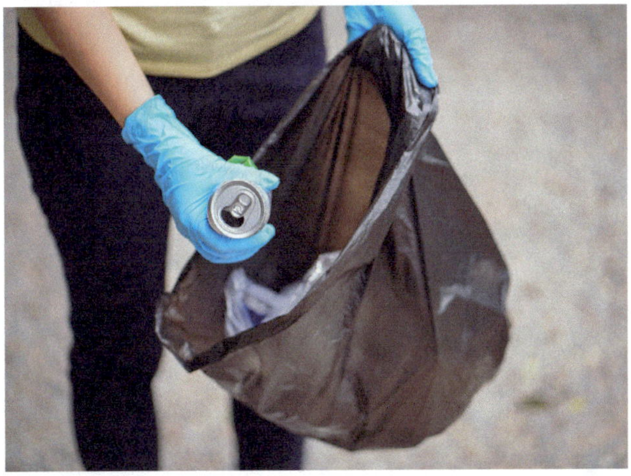

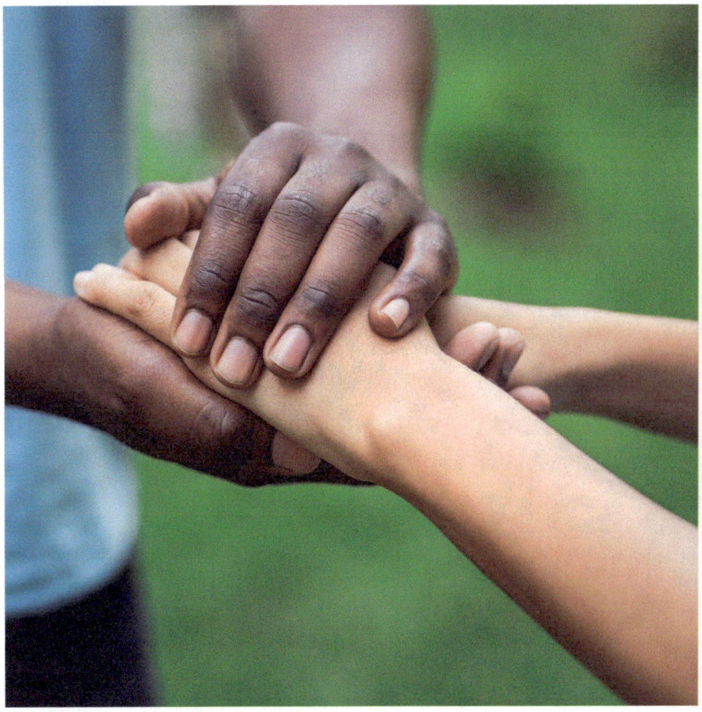

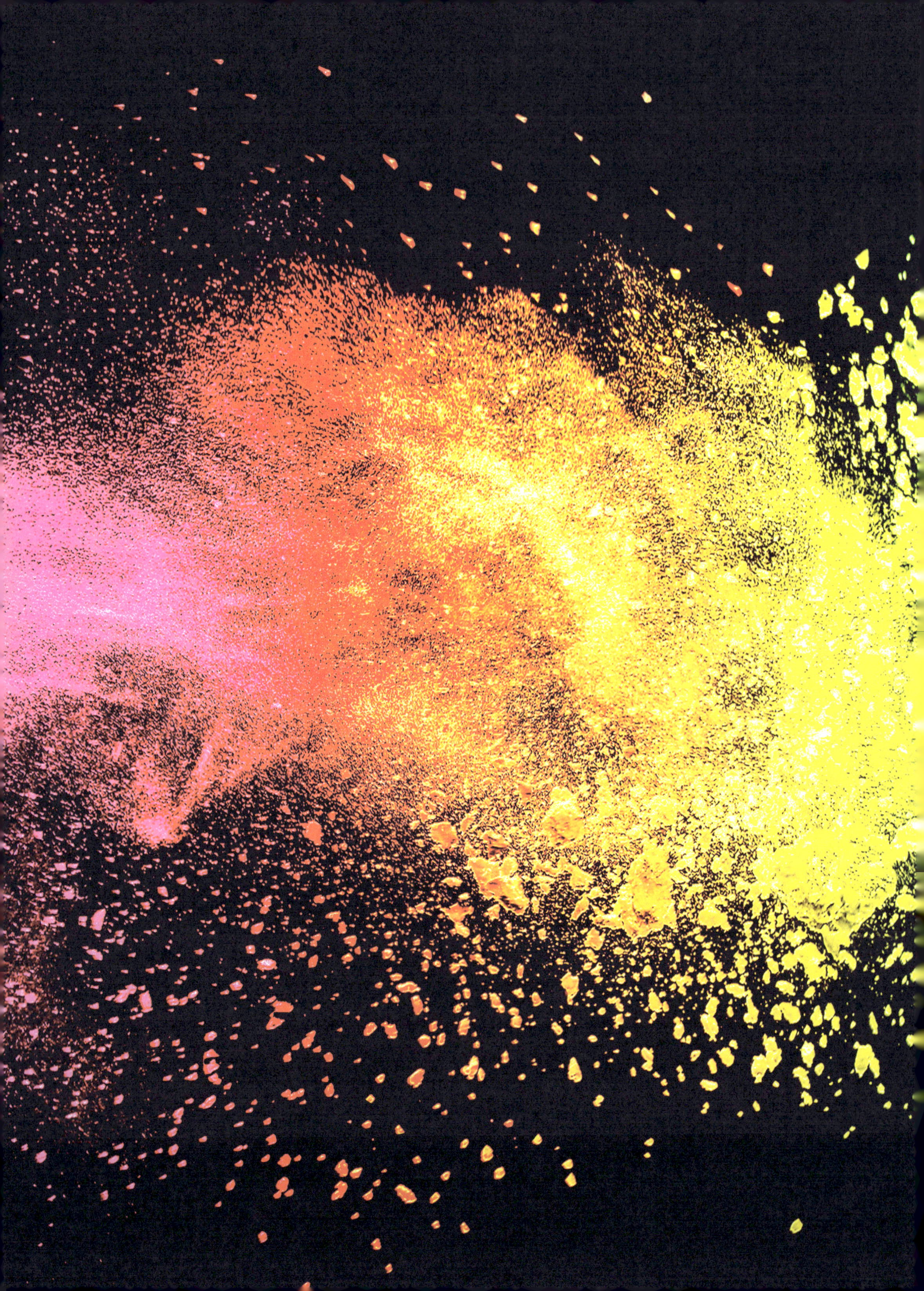

MY VISION BOARD PLANNER FOR 20_ _

HEALTH	SPIRITUALITY	WEALTH

TRAVEL	RELATIONSHIPS	HOBBIES/LIFESTYLE

THINGS I WANT TO TRY THIS YEAR

I AM	I AM
I AM	I AM

- Victorious
- Passionate
- Innovative
- Fearless
- Limitless
- Thriving

I AM	I AM
I AM	I AM

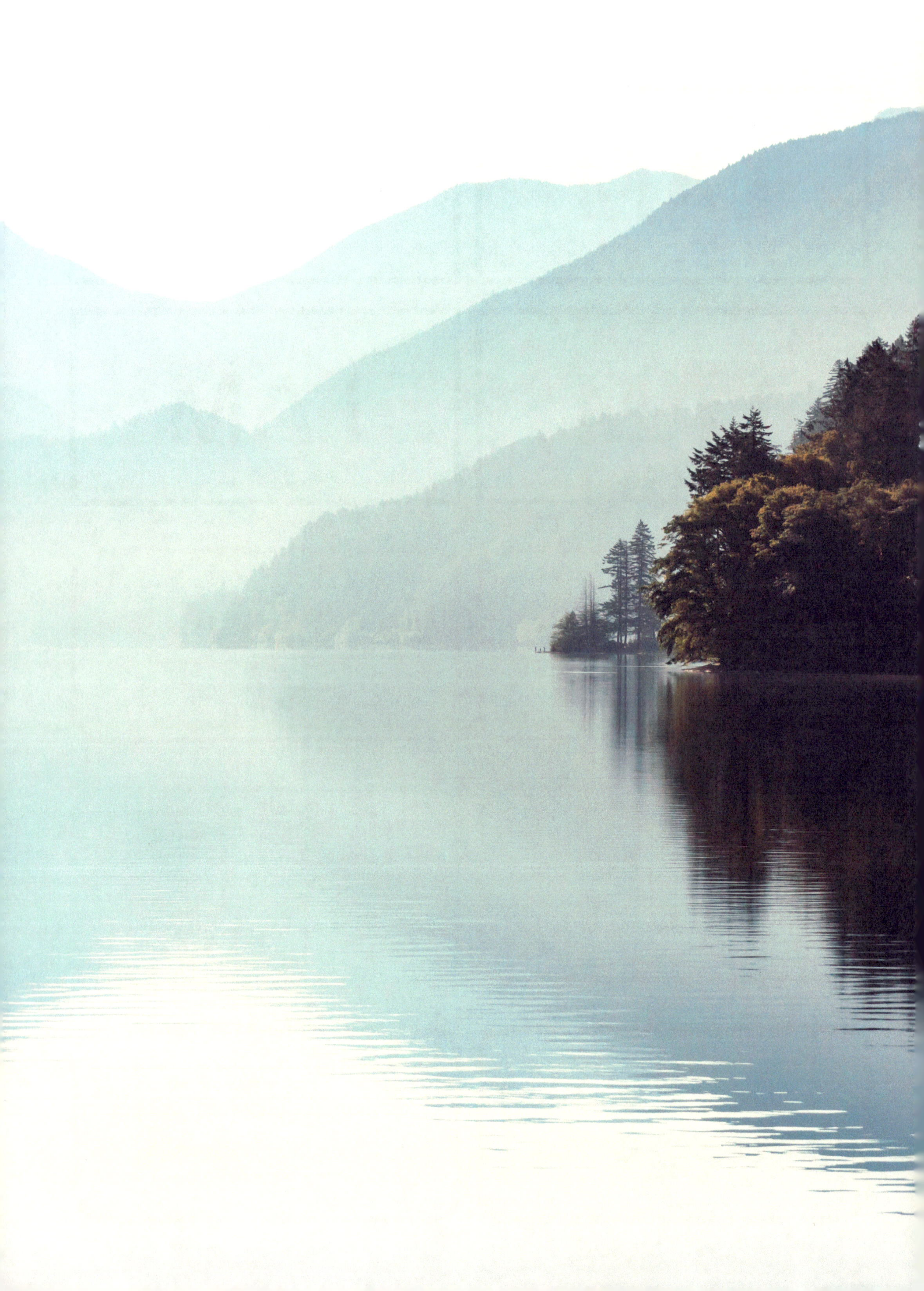

Bringing Your Vision to Life: Final Thoughts and Action Steps

"Do not be limited by other people's limited imaginations." - Dr. Mae Jemison

To conclude, I want to reiterate the importance of taking action toward your dreams. You have the power to create the life you want, and by using the tools and strategies provided in this book, you can make your dreams a reality.

Here are a few final tips to help you on your journey:

1. **Keep your vision board in a visible place** where you can see it every day. This will help you stay motivated and focused on your goals.
2. **Review your goals regularly** and adjust them as necessary. Life is constantly changing, and your goals should reflect that.
3. **Celebrate your successes**, no matter how small they may seem. Every step forward is a step closer to achieving your dreams.
4. **Don't be afraid to ask for help** or seek out resources to support you on your journey. You don't have to do it alone.

Remember, your dreams are within reach. With dedication, perseverance, and a clear vision of what you want, you can achieve anything you set your mind to.

So go out there and make it happen!

Made in the USA
Columbia, SC
28 December 2024